INSTRUCTOR'S MANUAL

GROUPS:
THEORY AND EXPERIENCE

Rodney W. Napier
Department of Psychoeducational Processes
Temple University

Matti K. Gershenfeld
Formerly Visiting Professor
Department of Educational Psychology
Temple University

Houghton Mifflin Company · Boston
Atlanta
Dallas
Geneva, Illinois
Hopewell, New Jersey
Palo Alto

Printed in the U.S.A.

ISBN: 0-395-14048-X

contents

introduction

This manual and the textbook represent an attempt to remedy the crucial lack of understandable theory and applied methods in the area of group processes for a wide variety of professionals in the field. Psychologists, teachers, counselors, community mental health workers, consultants, and many others involved in a broad range of group activities have discovered a dearth of information linking innovative laboratory practices to the conceptual viewpoints drawn from theory and research. Too frequently a few games, activities, or gimmicks are used to gain interest among those participating in a group. However, taken as they often are in isolation, they fail to integrate cognitive learning with experience in a meaningful manner. Too often the complexities of group life have been minimized into a simplistic formula which varies little from group to group. In some ways it can be likened to the doctor who prescribes penicillin for everything that ails a patient. Part of the problem, of course, stems from the fact that it has only been in the last decade that such great interest in group phenomena has occurred in so many diverse fields, and group facilitators are still seeking the kinds of information presented here.

Thus, our major purpose has been to broaden the repertoire of those working with groups of all types. By expanding both the theoretical and applied bases upon which the facilitator builds his behaviors, we hope to encourage new approaches to a wide variety of problems and issues. By providing an extensive range of choices we believe that assistance may be given to facilitators with differing styles and differing levels of skill. If, for example, a group is having difficulty understanding the conflicts of multiple membership, we have attempted to design a number of experiences that will focus directly on these problems and to provide the group with specific data to discuss. By relating the experience directly to theory and research there results a unique merging of cognitive information and experiential learning. But, again, because facilitators and their groups are at such different levels of readiness we have felt it necessary to provide a broad array of materials so that it would be possible to design the most appropriate learning experience.

We have organized the experience-based materials found in both the manual and the book in a clear, direct, and personal style. We are assuming that these materials are unfamiliar to the reader, and we have taken pains not only to develop clear steps for action but also to provide a rationale, questions for discussion, and, whenever possible, variations on the theme. We realize that not everyone will need such detailed guidance, but we have discovered that a great many useful designs are never used simply because those who might attempt them never gain a comfortable "feel" for them prior to their execution.

Why a Book and a Manual?

Originally the book was intended for facilitators with all the theoretical sections and exercises integrated under one cover. However, if the book were to be used by students or those with relatively little experience in the field, a number of the most valuable exercises might be inappropriate and even dangerous in their hands. For some of the exercises the discrimination of the teacher or facilitator is the crucial variable in their use. Similarly, many of the activities would be inappropriate if placed in the book since they depend on an element of surprise or timing, which would be reduced if the participants understood the outcomes of the design in advance. Thus, it became clear that some of the activities should be reserved for the professional facilitator who, with the proper discretion, can use them as keys to unlocking the appropriate learning process for a particular group at a particular time. Over 50 separate activities have been carefully selected and incorporated into this facilitator's manual.

However, because of our own understanding of the learning process, we believe that whenever possible an interdependent relationship sould be cultivated between the facilitator and the participants. Education is not something "done to" someone. With this in mind, it became all too obvious that there was no reason why those participating as learners about group process should not also have the opportunity to conduct a variety of activities either among themselves or with other groups. After all, what could provide better insights into how groups function than an opportunity to experience the impact of one's own intervention into a group? All at one time the participant becomes a diagnostician, designer, implementer, and evaluater. He becomes responsible for all facets of his learning. Therefore, we have attempted to reinforce the experiential model of the book by actually drawing the participant into another phase of the learning process. The 30 activities found at the end of the various theoretical chapters of the book are designed so that they can be easily understood and implemented by individuals with limited facilitative skills. This is not to suggest that they lack potency or are any less effective in stimulating interest than those found in the manual. Rather, we believe they will in many cases prove to be the most appropriate for use by the group, either in relation to its own development or because they will be easily replicated in other groups with little fear of adverse effects. It is essential that the manual activities and those in the text can be seen as integrally related. They should be used in any combination that will maximize the potential learnings for the group.

Because we have provided activities in the book, it was also necessary to provide some understanding of the facilitator's role. While no attempt was made to explore the facilitator's role in depth, a special appendix for facilitators has been included which may prove to be a valuable resource for "student" and "teacher" alike. It reviews certain basic assumptions relating to laboratory learning. In addition it offers a fairly complete overview of techniques often used to help facilitate group activity, to insure participation, and generally to induce a positive climate for learning. For the professional facilitator it may act as a reminder, and to the novice it will provide a useful introduction to the complexities underlying the role of a leader who attempts to help a group in its development. In either case it is a necessary supplement for providing a bridge between theory and application.

How to Use This Manual

The book and the manual provide a starting point. On the one hand the book may be used in a rather structured way, moving the group along topically through a variety of experiences in much the same manner as they are presented. Thus, patterns of communication, problems of perception, goals, membership, and norms follow in a logical order. Even the exercises are often ordered sequentially so that experiential learnings tend to be ordered to some degree in relation to the anticipated readiness of a group to undertake them. Theoretically, at least, the book and the accompanying activities are set up so as to maximize the cumulative impact of the various learnings. If this is the plan of attack being used by a facilitator, it seems reasonable that he would:

1. Read the book thoroughly and determine if the chapter sequence seems appropriate.
2. Familiarize himself with the activities at the end of each chapter in both the book and the manual.
3. Review the appendix for facilitators.
4. Begin to design an integrated series of experiences that would capitalize on the specific types of learnings which may be drawn from particular activities and which might underline or provide access to discussions of theoretical concepts or research.

This approach would be encouraged for those with limited experience and if there are rather severe restrictions such as time, goals, or group membership.

On the other hand, a more fluid approach to using the book is possible and, in many cases, preferable. Rather than a systematic, step-by-step journey through the text, an experienced facilitator will be able to diagnose specific areas of concern with which the group must deal if it is to move in a positive direction. By focusing the participants' attention on a particular theoretical section of the book and providing an appropriate activity, group members can gain immediate insight into an area of learning which will be of ultimate value to them merely because it is so timely. This approach, of course, requires maximum flexibility on the part of the facilitator and assumes a higher risk factor than the approach mentioned previously. Nevertheless, because it is focused directly on where the group is at a particular moment in time, it provides the best opportunity to use the resources of the group, to use data generated by the group, and to insure interest.

The most effective use of the book and manual will probably result when the facilitator is able to answer the questions, "Where is the group now? Where is it going and from where is it coming?" Methods for diagnosing the group in a manner that will help discover the answers to these questions are given in the facilitator's appendix and among the activities relating to problem solving, communication, and group development in particular.

Once such questions are answered, it is important to explore the variety of activities that might help to focus on the most salient issue(s) at hand. In addition to a general index in this manual, a brief description accompanies each of the activities and suggests where the activity tends to fit in relation to the book. It is important to notice that many of the activities, although placed in relation to a particular chapter in the book, are suggested for use in a variety of situations. Many leadership activities may be most appropriate when looking at membership or the normative structure and how it has been influenced by certain individuals. In one sense, the manual is a resource instrument to be used without rules and regulations. It is hoped that for many the book will be considered in a similar way.

Rod Napier
Matti Gershenfeld

1 exercises in perception and communication[1]

Overview of Exercises

1. *The Rasmussen Triangle–The Perception of Objective Facts* An example of how even the most concrete information can be distorted depending on the needs and psychological set of the participant.
2. *Rigidity and Inflexibility in Perception* A further demonstration of how we tend to be conditioned by our past experiences and expectations. These expectations tend to influence our ability to be open and flexible in the problem-solving process.
3. *The Rumor Game–Distortions of Verbal Perception* From the inability to view even mechanical events objectively, this exercise reveals how susceptible we are to verbal distortion based on previous experience, untested assumptions, and stereotypes we continue to hold.
4. *Hearing What We Wish to Hear* Just as we fail to listen without considerable distortion, this activity provides the opportunity for the participant to judge for himself how subjective he is when drawing information from reading material.
5. *Perceived Characteristics of a New Acquaintance* Moving in the direction of interpersonal behavior, the participant experiences how easily he sees what he wishes to see when meeting people for the first time. Our initial tendency to see what we wish to see may have a strong influence on the potential for any future relationship.
6. *The Old Lady–Young Lady: A Classic Example* Our tendency to project into others characteristics drawn from previous experience is clearly revealed in this activity. Selective perception is experienced by the participants in the light of real data that can be used to focus on their inclination to "shape reality" in relation to their own biases.
7. *Occupations of Famous People* This activity provides an interesting alternative to several activities described previously. It helps individuals to view how effectively our social background has colored our expectations.
8. *Distortions between the Ear, the Word, and the Hand* Our distortion of verbal messages is clearly revealed when we attempt to reproduce visually a

[1] It should be noted that Exercises 1–8 are, for the most part, built in a sequential manner. They focus on various aspects of perception and communication, moving from the concrete to the more abstract, from the mechanical to the more human characteristics, which reduce effective perception and, thus, communication. Used together or in part, they provide the facilitator with the opportunity to demonstrate in a dramatic fashion our inability to gather and sort a wide range of data without distortion.

description of a common object. In this case the participant is provided with the description of a common animal and asked to reproduce it.

9. *The Group Dynamics Tango: A Test of Verbal and Nonverbal Perception*   In human relationships we have a tendency to move toward or away from individuals because of how we read nonverbal cues. A grimace, a cast of the eye, or the tone of voice can have an immediate influence on us. With this exercise, individuals are provided the opportunity to test out this reality and demonstrate how sensitive (often overly so) we are to the nonverbal communication from others.

10. *The Observation of Nonverbal Behavior in a Group*   Moving from an understanding of how we respond to nonverbal cues in individuals, this activity helps focus on the degree to which we communicate our own feelings nonverbally, and how this influences the way others relate to us—even in a task-oriented situation.

11. *Defensive Communication*   While many of the previous activities fit directly into the theoretical presentations described in the book, this exercise allows the facilitator the opportunity to have the participants generate their own theory. Based on Gibb's model of defensive communication, it allows for an easy bridging of theory and reality.

12. *The Perception of Other Group Members: An Initial View*   One way to reduce our tendency to perceive selectively and become more aware of the factors that distort our ability to communicate effectively is by catching ourselves in the act of stereotyping others or responding to untested assumptions. This exercise provides a means of checking our perceptions in a relatively non-threatening manner.

13. *Perception Check for a More Advanced Group*   This exercise is designed to encourage groups that have been working together to analyze their own behaviors in a more open and direct fashion.

Other Suggested Exercises in the Manual Which Relate Directly to Problems of Communication and Perception[2]

Chapter 2	4. Reference Groups—Who Am I?
Chapter 4	1. Hidden Agenda Role Play
	2. Dimensions of Cooperation
Chapter 5	5. 64 Squares—Different Leadership Styles
Chapter 6	A number of the problem-solving activities depend to some degree on how well individuals are able to separate distortions from reality. Thus, they would fit nicely into the perspective of this chapter. These include:
	1. The Horse Trade
	1. The Multiple Dot Test

[2] All of these suggestions are found in the manual. Other equally interesting alternatives will be found in the book at the end of various chapters.

AN EDUCATION FOR FREEDOM

Methods for destroying individual freedom are being developed rapidly, and the pressures to adopt them are becoming increasingly powerful. We can be educated for freedom– much better educated for freedom than we are at present. In coping with any complex human situation, we must consider all the relevant factors. Preventive legislation might do some good, but if the great impersonal forces now menacing freedom continue to gather momentum, they cannot do much good for very long.

Furthermore, an ethical system based on a fairly realistic appraisal of the data of experiences is likely to do more good than harm. But, the effects of false and pernicious propaganda cannot be neutralized except by a thorough training in the art of analyzing its techniques and seeing through its sophistries. An education for freedom (and for the love and intelligence which are at once the condition and results of freedom) must be, among other things, an education in the proper use of the language.

Finally, we know that in a very large and complex society democracy is almost meaningless except in relation to autonomous groups of manageable size; nonetheless more and more of every nation's affairs are managed by the bureaucrats of big government and big business. If a revolution takes place, it will be due in part to business, in part to forces over which even the most powerful rulers have very little control, and in part to the incompetence of those rulers and their inability to make effective use of the mind-manipulating instruments with which science and technology have supplied and will go on supplying the would-be tyrant.

Perhaps the forces that now menace freedom are too strong to be resisted for very long. It is still our duty to do whatever we can to resist them.

In fact, the story is a mixture of three separate essays and makes very little sense. But, since we have a need to make sense, to bring order into a confusing world, the tendency will be for the participants to pick out a piece of information that makes sense to them and use this as the essence of the story. Nearly everyone in the group will select a different point. These should be briefly recorded in front of the group. Obviously there can be no right or wrong, but individuals will speak with great certainty about their responses. The learnings are self-evident, but it is important that the participant does not feel duped or ignorant for shaping reason and meaning into the story. These interpretations are based on our present needs and past experiences and it is reality, or what we do with the reality, that becomes the most important question. Any short but rather complicated article with several points of view may serve the same purposes.

5. Perceived Characteristics of a New Acquaintance

A stranger to the group is given its attention for perhaps 5 minutes while he makes an announcement or discusses something of general interest. He then leaves. The participants are then asked to write down the three things they remember best another if necessary. The group has 3 or 4 minutes to ponder the problem, and the facilitator then asks for the number who successfully solved it within the given limitations. Usually it can be anticipated that no more than 5 percent will solve it and, often, no one discovers the solution. But why not? Expectations, past perceptions, an inability to move from a limited visual perspective, and a rigid inflexibility in the problem-solving process are a few of the reasons. Just as the Russian worker was able to convince himself that he would die, likewise moving outside the confined limits of the square brought failure in what should have been a simple task.

3. The Rumor Game—Distortion of Verbal Perception

Facing a group with its own inclination to distort verbal messages can be a humorous but, at the same time, an enlightening experience. This exercise is an extension of the old rumor (telephone) game we used to play as children. Six volunteers are asked to leave the room. The remaining individuals are asked to be "detectives." The plan is to have one individual return to the room and listen carefully to a brief story. He is then told to repeat the story as exactly as possible to the next individual in front of the group. The second then repeats it to the third, the third to the fourth, and so on. Meanwhile the observing group has the task of noting exactly where distortions develop and why. When the last person has been called in and told the story by person number five, he repeats it back to the total group, and the facilitator writes it on the board (often by this time it is only a few words). There are a hundred possible reasons for the distortions, and the detectives should have ample time to share observations and theories. For example, some people "choke" in front of a group, some project "rightness" and "wrongness" into the story, others add humor to compensate for their nervousness, and still others personalize the account. The distortions are often hilarious, but the implications are not and should be underlined. Rereading the account can act as a useful point of summary and bring closure to the activity. The story should be relatively short (100 to 150 words), not very complicated, but with a story line that evokes interest and involves activity among people. The easier it is for individuals to associate themselves with the story (perhaps to be a bit threatened by it), the more predictable will be the distortions.

4. Hearing What We Wish to Hear

The fact that we hear what we need to hear can be revealed quite simply. The group is asked to listen carefully to an essay concerning education and freedom (topics which are close to each of us). At the end of the brief account, the facilitator will ask a number of individuals to condense the information into a few sentences. The essay follows:

reads the number that corresponds to the one on their paper. At least 10 or 12 different responses can be expected among a group of 25 to 50 participants. The distribution of responses often shows several answers agreed to by large numbers of individuals. Often it is helpful to have a few of the individuals with widely divergent responses discuss their particular approach. The implications are usually obvious, and the point need not be belabored, although the facilitator might have to add to the possible reasons for so many responses.

2. Rigidity and Inflexibility in Perception

The group is told the story of the poor Russian laborer (he just happened to be Russian) whose job was to clean out box cars in a railroad yard. One evening during a break, he slipped into an empty freezer car which was being aired out, piled some straw in a corner, and proceeded to catch a few winks. He was awakened when the door was slammed shut by a yard policeman who had not noticed him in the car. Being philosophical about the plight of his life anyway, he decided to record for posterity the process of death as it slowly crept up on him. There appeared to be no escape unless the guards returned unexpectedly before morning. As the night wore on, the notes he scraped on the wall become less and less coherent, his fingers numbed, and his breath came in short gasps. But he continued to write and hoped that his short history of impending death would be of interest. At some point in the early hours of the morning he scratched his last message: "I can no longer grasp this stick, there is no air to breathe . . . ." In the morning, when the heavy door was pulled open, he was found dead, lying there still clutching his stick. The temperature inside was 55 degrees, and there was plenty of oxygen. The facilitator should let the group mull over the meaning of this event for a few minutes and share the reasons for the unnecessary death and its implications.

Then, he indicates that he would like the members to solve a rather easy problem, again, by themselves. There are nine dots in a figure (a large and easily readable reproduction should be placed on a blackboard), and it is necessary for the participants to connect all of the dots with *four* straight lines. At no time are they allowed to take their pencils away from the paper, and they may not retrace any line before beginning the next. Thus, although there are to be four lines (or less), they must be connected with one following after the other. Of course, the lines may cross one

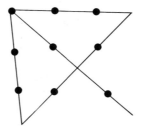

A Series of Brief Experiences in Selective Perception

The following exercises deal directly with our limited ability to perceive objectively a situation and report it back without considerable distortion. It does not matter whether the stimuli being presented are visual or auditory in nature because our needs and a variety of other factors twist the particular event. None of the exercises presented here need take more than 20 or 30 minutes, although, of course, discussion on any one could extend much longer if desired. The idea is to put together a series of experiences that highlight for a particular group certain learnings that need particular attention. Since it is easy to discount the results of any one exercise, a sequence of four or five tends to drive the point home effectively. It should be noted that the examples move from those that are concrete, physical, visual, and more or less objective to those that are less specific, more obscure, and more vulnerable to distortion because of the human variable. The designs are not "tricks," and what occurs is a result of the participant "inputs."

1. The Rasmussen Triangle — The Perception of Objective Facts

The participants are given the directions by the facilitator (a little humor and tension can stimulate involvement): "You have three minutes to complete the following test. Please do not talk to your neighbor. Write your response on a piece of paper. You are to count the number of triangles in the diagram. Again, keep your eyes on your own paper. You may begin." The test atmosphere, although obviously a put-on, has a remarkable influence on most groups. Members are given a large piece of newsprint or a blackboard on which they write the numbers from 1 through 25 in a long column. Then they are asked to raise their hands when the facilitator

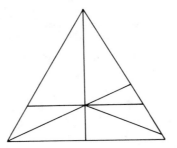

reads the number that corresponds to the one on their paper. At least 10 or 12 different responses can be expected among a group of 25 to 50 participants. The distribution of responses often shows several answers agreed to by large numbers of individuals. Often it is helpful to have a few of the individuals with widely divergent responses discuss their particular approach. The implications are usually obvious, and the point need not be belabored, although the facilitator might have to add to the possible reasons for so many responses.

2. Rigidity and Inflexibility in Perception

The group is told the story of the poor Russian laborer (he just happened to be Russian) whose job was to clean out box cars in a railroad yard. One evening during a break, he slipped into an empty freezer car which was being aired out, piled some straw in a corner, and proceeded to catch a few winks. He was awakened when the door was slammed shut by a yard policeman who had not noticed him in the car. Being philosophical about the plight of his life anyway, he decided to record for posterity the process of death as it slowly crept up on him. There appeared to be no escape unless the guards returned unexpectedly before morning. As the night wore on, the notes he scraped on the wall become less and less coherent, his fingers numbed, and his breath came in short gasps. But he continued to write and hoped that his short history of impending death would be of interest. At some point in the early hours of the morning he scratched his last message: "I can no longer grasp this stick, there is no air to breathe . . . ." In the morning, when the heavy door was pulled open, he was found dead, lying there still clutching his stick. The temperature inside was 55 degrees, and there was plenty of oxygen. The facilitator should let the group mull over the meaning of this event for a few minutes and share the reasons for the unnecessary death and its implications.

Then, he indicates that he would like the members to solve a rather easy problem, again, by themselves. There are nine dots in a figure (a large and easily readable reproduction should be placed on a blackboard), and it is necessary for the participants to connect all of the dots with *four* straight lines. At no time are they allowed to take their pencils away from the paper, and they may not retrace any line before beginning the next. Thus, although there are to be four lines (or less), they must be connected with one following after the other. Of course, the lines may cross one

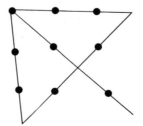

A Series of Brief Experiences in Selective Perception

The following exercises deal directly with our limited ability to perceive objectively a situation and report it back without considerable distortion. It does not matter whether the stimuli being presented are visual or auditory in nature because our needs and a variety of other factors twist the particular event. None of the exercises presented here need take more than 20 or 30 minutes, although, of course, discussion on any one could extend much longer if desired. The idea is to put together a series of experiences that highlight for a particular group certain learnings that need particular attention. Since it is easy to discount the results of any one exercise, a sequence of four or five tends to drive the point home effectively. It should be noted that the examples move from those that are concrete, physical, visual, and more or less objective to those that are less specific, more obscure, and more vulnerable to distortion because of the human variable. The designs are not "tricks," and what occurs is a result of the participant "inputs."

1. The Rasmussen Triangle — The Perception of Objective Facts

The participants are given the directions by the facilitator (a little humor and tension can stimulate involvement): "You have three minutes to complete the following test. Please do not talk to your neighbor. Write your response on a piece of paper. You are to count the number of triangles in the diagram. Again, keep your eyes on your own paper. You may begin." The test atmosphere, although obviously a put-on, has a remarkable influence on most groups. Members are given a large piece of newsprint or a blackboard on which they write the numbers from 1 through 25 in a long column. Then they are asked to raise their hands when the facilitator

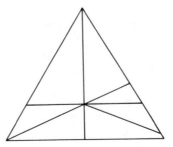

about the individual, those things that characterize him best. Although they are not asked to sign the paper, they are requested to include certain other information about themselves, such as age, sex, occupation, religion, or other facts that might provide a basis for patterns that develop in the group's observation of the individual. While the group turns to other business, someone tabulates the data. First, the most common characteristics are noted. Second, extremes are reported. For example, some individuals will remember clothes, others physical mannerisms, and still others attitudinal or behavioral characteristics. Finally, the data can be analyzed according to the make-up of the group. Did different age groups notice different characteristics, or were there differences in responses of men and women? A 10- or 15-minute presentation and discussion of the data can open the door to a wide range of issues and stimulate involvement at more significant levels. It is important that the person discussed has been made fully cognizant of the activity and is willing to cooperate in it. Also, the participants should know of this willingness before they proceed with their observations and later discussion.

6. The Old–Young Lady: A Classic Example

Originally drawn in 1905 (the artist was W. E. Hill drawing for *Puck*), the ambiguous picture of the Old Lady–Young Lady composite has been used in innumerable psychological experiments in this country for four decades. It provides a fascinating example of our need to create a particular figure ground relationship out of an

ambiguous stimulus. Depending on the time available and the objectives, there are a variety of potential exercises that can be developed. Here is only one:

The large group is divided into subgroups of from five to seven. They are told that they are on the board of selection of a country club, a wealthy benefactor of the club has told them that he has a friend moving to town who doesn't know anyone, and he would greatly appreciate it if they would accept her membership on his recommendation. He has brought a picture of her, and he has not thought it necessary to bring additional information. The committee members thank him and tell him that they will let him know.

At this point, each group is given a 20- or 30-second look at a large reproduction of the picture (an overhead projector is another possibility) and told to individually answer the following questions as best they can from what they have seen. (It is very important that the group is primed to play the game and use their imaginations in working at the task). The questions are:

1. How old is the person?
2. What is her social class (upper, upper-middle, middle, lower-middle or lower)?
3. How much education has the person had?
4. What is her occupation, or what do you imagine she has done?
5. From her appearance, would you trust her?

The groups are then instructed that they will have 10 minutes to agree on a single response for each category to be reported back to the total group. Time is a factor since there are many other applications to process.

On a large blackboard, the group leader draws a grid upon which he can record the responses of each group to the questions. He then pools the groups for their answers, again stressing only one answer for each. If there are eight groups, one can anticipate an age range to be from the early twenties to over fifty. Responses cover all levels of social class and education. Occupations usually create quite a stir as housewife, maid, dancer, sales girl, prostitute, and many others are expressed. Finally, it often happens that most of the groups do not trust the individual. Innocent until proven guilty? Frequently we find it much easier to protect outselves through mistrust.

The discussion should generate spontaneously from the data as the group begins to explore its own stereotypes and the possible reasons for them. At some point during the discussion it is useful to show the group the two images that comprise the picture. A second level of discussion can easily develop out of the reality that group pressure forced many individuals to change in the direction of the group even though their perceptions were just as correct. A show of hands of how many saw the old or the young lady can be used as a starter for having the group look at its own problem-solving behavior and the power relations that existed during the session. The group, however, may not be ready for such a discussion and, if done prematurely, it will benefit little from this phase of the discussion.

7. Occupations of Famous People

An exercise related to the one just described can prove interesting. The group leader selects eight full-sized pictures (at least 9″ by 11″) and places them in a row so that all of the participants can see all of the pictures at one time. Six of the eight pictures should be of important people who are known and respected throughout the country, but who might not be easily recognized: an astronaut relaxing at golf, the Prime Minister of Australia swimming, a famous scientist gardening, or a professional basketball player playing a pick-up game on a slum playground. In addition, two people of ill-repute should be selected, such as a member of the Mafia standing by his boat, or a convicted killer in some informal setting. At this point, a list of 12 occupations or distinguishing characteristics of 12 men are posted (i.e., prime minister, killer, basketball player) so that 6 of the roles or occupations are of people with negative connotations and 6 represent people who are clearly respected. As in the previous exercise, a group-questioning procedure may be developed. Thus, individuals in small groups of about five could first attempt to match the right picture to the man independent of the group. Later the small group would attempt to reach agreement and share its responses with the large group. The key here is to encourage individuals to free-associate with the pictures and allow their stereotypes to move them. This is, after all, what we usually do. The discussion is built on the stereotypes of the group and of individuals, both those admitted and those repressed (but later drawn out during the discussion).

8. Distortions between the Ear, the Word, and the Hand

An exercise that provides a nice change of pace as well as a bit of levity involves tapping into the artistic ability of the participants. They are given a piece of paper and a pencil, told to listen carefully to a description of a well-known animal, and then to sketch it as best they can. It should be emphasized that perfect art is not the goal, but rather some facsimile of the creature. The facilitator gives the description as follows:

> It is small, with a long nose, ears, and a tail, the latter being naked and prehensile. The opposable first hind toe is clawless, and the tip is expanded into a flat pad. The other digits all bear claws. The best-known species is about the size of a cat, gray in color, with wooly fur.[1]

A brief sampling of the works of art will reveal an enormous range of both artistic ability and figural distortions as individuals concentrate on certain aspects of the animal (long nose, prehensile tail, etc.) and build the animal around it. The activity

[3]This description is taken from the *Encyclopedia Britannica,* and the idea for the exercise is from: D. Fabun, ed., Communications, *Kaiser Aluminum 23*(3), 1965, 34. (The animal is an opossum.)

is used to underline points already made and to help a group begin to laugh at itself and at its own frailties.

Individuals distort what they perceive, and groups, if undisciplined and not practiced, will tend to multiply these distortions. An unending supply of exercises can be cultivated out of everyday experiences. For example, take a picture of nearly any scene and have individuals or small groups describe it after it is taken from view. What is left in the description? What is left out? What is basically altered? What can be taken with certainty from the picture? After this activity the facilitator may ask: What are the assumptions left untested by us in order to reinforce a particular impression or stereotype? The simplest data can provide rich questions and insights. In summary, it cannot be stressed too greatly that sequencing these activities in terms of the needs of a particular group is perhaps the most important part of the program. Otherwise, they may look like gimmicks.

9. The Group Dynamics Tango: A Test of Verbal and Nonverbal Perception

Objectives

To illustrate that people hear words and perceive situations differently
To create an awareness that what is threatening is often not determined by the sender but by the receiver

Setting

This exercise goes a step beyond the simple verbal feedback in the Three-Stage Rocket (see Exercise 3 in the textbook). To undertake it, the group must be ready to begin looking at the many subtle variables that influence the communication between two people. It requires members who have expressed some interest in sharing their personal perceptions of one another in the communication process. The activity itself requires that group members sit around the room leaving a space of 20 feet clear in the center. Two members are asked to volunteer (in some cases two individuals who have minor communication problems with each other are most useful). They are instructed to stand in the middle of the room, facing each other, about 8 feet apart.

Action

The two participants are asked to involve themselves in a conversation in which they have some disagreement. One person begins by simply making a statement. The other person listens carefully. If he in any way feels threatened by the words, tone of voice, or other nonverbal behavior, he is to take a step backwards. If, on the other hand, he feels accepted, well received, or supported, he takes a step forward. If he has no positive or negative response, he merely stays where he is. Both participants continue to carry on their conversation and proceed to move as they feel the urge. The aim is to get the two together, not necessarily in ideas, but through a mutual acceptance of each other. The group observing is instructed to watch the movement of the two individuals to see if they can determine what it was that moved a particular individual forward or back. After 5 or 10 minutes, it is useful to discuss what they and the group saw happening and why. Then, another couple can try the exercise. Also, if there is enough space, the group can be broken into pairs and try the activity on their own, later discussing with their partner their perceptions of what happened. A later sharing of insights among the total group may be helpful.

Variation

If a group is involved in a discussion and would like to add another dimension to its "listening process," it is possible for the whole group to take part in the exercise. As a person talks, members quietly move their chairs backward or forward as the message they receive, directly or indirectly, from the individual is perceived as positive or negative. After 20 or 30 minutes, time should be spent discussing the present position of the group and the movement that people noticed during the exercise. Again, it is important that the group desire to explore this aspect of communication and that the activity not be imposed upon them; otherwise it will be difficult for them to remain serious during the activity. A group of more than 20 becomes a bit difficult to manage, although given space, it is theoretically possible for a group of any size.

10. The Observation of Nonverbal Behavior in a Group

Objectives

To alert the participants to dimensions of communication other than verbal
To increase the participants' awareness of their own nonverbal behavior in a group

Rationale

Few people deny the important influence nonverbal behavior can have on communication. The problem is, however, that we are often too busy to realize the impact it is having. Taking time to observe nonverbal communication at length can help provide the facilitator with a new perspective of a group and broaden his understanding of individual behavior as well.

Setting

This exercise is often very effective with individuals who do not know one another, although it can also be an interesting experience for groups in which the participants are acquainted. The large group is divided into two pairs with from 7 to 11 or 12 members in each group. Members are given tags with numbers on them. There will be a number 1 in each group, a number 2 in each group, and so on. Ten chairs are placed in a circle with another chair behind each inner chair (assuming 10 in each group). The two groups are briefed separately for the task. Both the inner group *A* and the outer group *B* are given the same initial set of instructions, as follows:

> The country is under the threat of nuclear war. In this part of the country, there are very few shelters where people could sustain themselves for a period of 6 months– the time estimated it would take before land would be safe for reoccupation. A group of prominent elder citizens has been chosen to help determine which of various individuals should be given access to particular bomb shelters (the selectors have indicated that they would prefer not to compete for such openings). For one of these shelters, the list has been reduced from 200 down to 10. The elders are meeting now to further reduce the group to five. They have decided that the best procedure would be to rank-order the 10 individually and then discuss their reasons and arrive at a group decision. Those being considered are (ages are in parentheses):
>
> > A famous musician (47)
> > A nuclear physicist (51)
> > A young woman, six months pregnant (23)
> > A policeman (41)
> > An accountant (28) (husband of the young woman)
> > A nun-schoolteacher (31)
> > A professional athlete (35)
> > A female dancer-entertainer (28)
> > A medical student– Negro (25)
> > A priest (56)

Group *B* is told that in addition to having an opportunity to be involved in the problem solving (as an elder group), they will begin by observing group *A* for 15 minutes. They will pay particular attention to the person with the same number as they are wearing. Their objective is to build a picture of their number counterpart by accumulating as much nonverbal data as they can in the 15 minutes. They would then have an opportunity to paint a verbal picture of that person: tone of voice, eye contact, posture, gestures of every kind (but not physical afflictions).

Action

The two groups assemble, and the task for *A* is briefly reviewed. Participants are told that they will have 15 minutes; then group *B* spends 15 minutes in the middle discussing the same problem. The discussion usually builds up quite rapidly, and most individuals actively participate.

After 15 minutes, the discussion is halted, and the group members pair off according to the same number. The *B* member of the dyad shares his data with his partner in as descriptive a fashion as possible. No value judgments should be made.

After 5 or 10 minutes, the *B* group is asked to assemble in the middle, the *A* group is moved to the side, and the facilitator gives the following instructions: "It is now your turn to observe group *B*. This time join forces with another member of your own group. For example, numbers two and five will both observe numbers two and five in the other group. The task, however, is a little different. Instead of observing all nonverbal behavior, observe particularly those nonverbal behaviors that *a*) push people away from the individual (again it could be a look, the tone of voice, a withdrawing physically from the group, etc.), and *b*, those nonverbal behaviors that draw people to the person being observed (a smile, eye contact, position in his chair, etc.)."

At the next break the observers will share their information with the two they have been watching in a group of four. Again the information should be reported in a nonevaluative manner based on behavioral examples.

At this point, group *A* is asked to return to the center and spend another 10 minutes discussing their decisions. *B* is simply told to observe the nonverbal behavior influencing the group. After 10 minutes the groups switch, and group *B* has an opportunity to complete the procedure. Group *A* is also asked to view the general nonverbal behavior influencing the group.

Discussion

New groups of four members each (two from each group) should be formed to sift through the enormous amount of nonverbal data generated and to begin forming some conclusions about which kinds seem to be facilitative and which actually hinder the development of a discussion. These are then shared with members of both groups. If time permits, it is important to give the groups an opportunity to share a variety of other learnings from the simulation of the bomb shelter itself. Sharing other learnings is very provocative and raises many issues related to group process (norms, membership, decision making).

11. Defensive Communication

Objectives

To help the group generate a greater awareness of those characteristics of individual behavior that create defensiveness in ourselves and others

Setting

This activity usually follows a period of intensive activity when group members have been involved in solving a particularly difficult problem or have encountered conflict in other ways. Groups of five or six, which have not been, for the most part, together on the previous task, are developed. They are told: "There is seldom a group in which we fail to find behaviors that do not make us or the other participants defensive. At times, we ourselves are the culprits. In the next hour you have the following task:

1. List as many specific behaviors as you can that you are sure raise your own defenses or those of others.
2. Describe some of those defensive behaviors.
3. In some manner develop a theory of defensive behavior that can be presented to the larger group (this assumes a total group of no more than about 40 or 45). You may wish to portray your theory graphically through a diagram or a skit. The method is up to you. The presentation should not, however, take over five minutes."

At least 2 hours should be allowed for the total exercise since an hour may not be enough for the groups to develop their ideas in a satisfactory manner. Also, at least a half hour is needed for the presentations with time for subsequent discussion. Newsprint and magic markers should be available for each group for the presentation.

Action

The facilitator should move among the groups making certain that no members become bogged down because of not understanding the task, or because the concept of theory building has them stumped. The idea is simply to have them share their views and in some manner organize these views in a systematic way for the other group members. Sophistication is not necessarily the essence of a good product. The facilitator may wish to present a brief theory session of his own at the tail end of the session to show how the group was successfully able to incorporate the major ideas of other theorists in the field by pooling their resources and experience. Gibb's (1961) theory, in which he outlines behaviors that facilitate and inhibit a supportive climate, provides a useful supplement.

DEFENSIVE CLIMATES		SUPPORTIVE CLIMATES
Evaluation	vs.	Description
Control	vs.	Problem orientation
Strategy	vs.	Spontaneity
Neutrality	vs.	Empathy
Superiority	vs.	Equality
Certainty	vs.	Provisionalism

Perception Check

12. The Perception of Other Group Members: An Initial View

Objectives

To reveal how our own needs help to distort our initial view of other group members.

Setting

With a bit of flexibility, this exercise can be used with groups at various stages of development. It is particularly interesting during the initial meeting of a new group. Groups of between four and six are formed. The facilitator gives the following instruction: "Briefly get to know each other by discussing who you are for this group and perhaps what your strengths and weaknesses are in working with groups."

Members are given 15 minutes to respond among themselves. This situation provides a wide range of possible responses on the part of the various members; some are open and candid while others are less expressive of their ideas and feelings.

Action

After 15 or 20 minutes in the original discussion, each person is given a piece of paper on which they will answer the following questions:

1. On a one-to-seven scale with seven being high and one being low, rank how open and honest you were during this discussion. If you did not feel very open or honest with the group, write in a one, two, or three; if you did feel relatively open, write in a five, six, or seven.
2. Now, rank the level of the other group members (as a whole) in the same manner. If you feel the group was sharing in an open and honest fashion, you will want to rank it high, etc.

Members do not sign the paper, but they indicate whether they are male or female at the top of the page.

All the papers are collected, and then the groups spend about 15 minutes discussing their responses in as much depth as they wish and, perhaps, also discuss why the two questions were asked. They can use this time to get to know one another even better.

Data Analysis

The facilitator draws two long lines on the board and graphs the answers by marking them along a one-to-seven scale, using white chalk for men and blue for women. He makes a side note of the number of times an individual will rank the group lower than himself in openness and honesty. Usually, there is a distinct difference between the two questions. Most often the women are willing to be more candid about themselves, but see the group as holding back. Also, people usually see themselves as more open than they see the group. If this occurs, the implications are very important, since if we see others being less candid than ourselves, the tendency is to risk less and be even less open. In turn this has a similar effect on the others, thus slowly eroding the level of trust in the group and creating an atmosphere of more rather than less suspicion.

13. Perception Check for a More Advanced Group

Objectives

To help a person perceive how well individuals are hearing him and the degree to which others in the group are being listened to

Setting

This exercise is designed as a means of encouraging groups that have been working together to analyze their own behaviors in a more open and direct fashion. It is meant to confront the group with one important aspect of communication, one having a great deal to do with how accepted we are in that group. It should only be attempted when individuals reveal a willingness to look more closely at personal data about themselves and how they communicate. The group is told:

> Whenever you are working in a group there are some people that really listen to you. They listen a little harder because they agree with you, like you, or feel what you say has meaning and perhaps relevance. Write down the names of the two people (depending on the size of the group, this could be three or even four) who really listen to you. Then write down the names of the two people in the group whom you listen to the most.

Action

The participants write down the names: who listens to me the most (2) and those I listen to the most (2). Each person reads his responses, and they are tabulated (it is also possible for one person to read them all, thus reducing some of the tensions).

If a person is listened to by both those who he thinks listen to him, he receives 2 points. If only one person predicted as listening to him the most actually does, only 1 point is given.

Discussion

What about the people in the group who score 0?
Who in the group are listened to by the most people? Why?
Who in the group are listened to the least?
Why does this occur in this particular group, and how is it possible to alter this distribution—for individuals and for the group?

Once members begin to ask the "why" question, they become involved in describing personal behavior. But, again, if the group is not ready to face these kinds of questions, the exercise is premature.

2 exercises in membership

Overview of Exercises

1,2. *Initial Membership Experiences* The best way to experience the tensions that result when we enter a new group is by creating the elements of a new group and allowing ourselves the opportunity to look at our natural response to the new situation. Considerable attention is given to the kinds of feelings generated.

3. *Conflicts of Multiple Memberships—Alter Ego Exercise* This activity enables the participants to see how much our feelings and behaviors in a group can be determined by our relationship to other groups and the kinds of expectations these multiple memberships create in us.

4. *Reference Groups—Who Am I?* We bring with us to each group roles and expectations from a variety of other groups. In this exercise the focus is on individual differences based on previous experiences. Differences in individual value systems are easily perceived as influences on the priorities of the different group members as the group developed.

5. *Increasing Attractiveness of the Group—High Status—Low Status* The influence of one's status in a group in terms of acceptance and rejection and the methods used by individuals to cope with each are explored.

6. *How Can Attractiveness of a Group Be Increased? The Quiet One Exercise* An implicit or explicit issue in many groups revolves around individuals who do not actively participate. This activity opens the issue and its implications for both active and passive individuals. The resulting discussion may help the group to reappraise its own membership criteria.

Other Suggested Exercises in the Manual which Relate Directly to the Issue of Membership in a Group

Chapter 1	5.	Perceived Characteristics of a New Acquaintance
	6.	The Old Lady–Young Lady
	10.	The Observation of Nonverbal Behavior in a Group (The simulation design used is particularly stimulating and polarizes people along value lines immediately.)
Chapter 3	3.	Effects of Group Pressures toward Uniformity
Chapter 5	1.	Task-Maintenance Exercise
	2.	Functional Roles of Membership
Chapter 6	5.	The Hollow Square
	7.	The Nonzero Sum Game
	13.	Role Reversal: Means of Unblocking a Polarized Group
Chapter 7	2.	Tower Building

1. Initial Membership Experiences—Uniqueness of Individual Entering a Group

The uniqueness of the individual is apparent in his approach to others, to problems, and to life. Each member does not come into a new group with a *tabula rasa* on which the events of the group will be written. He comes with some expectations for his experience in that group. His expectations may be clear or hazy; he may be looking forward to it or dreading it; he may be deeply concerned or indifferent; he may feel comfortable in a new situation or anxious; he may feel "in" or "out."

Objective

To help participants to understand that each person comes to a new situation in his own way, and with his own expectations and unique behaviors.

Setting

This exercise can be performed by any number of participants. It is most effective if used as an initial experience.

Preparations

A room should be arranged so that some of the chairs and tables are conducive to group discussions; but some chairs should be placed individually, i.e., somewhat isolated, and the room should not be ordered or symmetrically arranged. The room should be darkened (lights turned out or shades drawn).

Action

All the participants go into the hall outside of the room. The facilitator asks that each close his eyes just before reentering the room. He leads each person through the doorway. The facilitator instructs all to mill around. After a few moments, he says, "Will each person find a place for himself?" He repeats the instruction. (Since participants are milling around, they will interpret the last instruction as meaning a chair or a sitting place on the floor).

If members cannot find a place (if all the chairs near them are occupied), the facilitator will guide the person to a chair or the area of a chair. Those who occupy the isolated chairs may be guided to a chair with a group of people. Those who resist help should be left alone. Those sitting at tables are asked to "get to know one another, but still with your eyes closed."

The facilitator waits about 15 minutes. He then turns on the lights so that people can see with whom they are sitting, and react to each other as to their expectations of that person.

Discussion

If possible, all should sit in one group for discussion. The following questions are posed: How did you feel when you came into the darkened room? How did you feel when you bumped into someone—something? How did you respond? What did you do when you milled around? Did you move around, stay near walls, move near or away from people, hardly move? How did you find your place? Was it easy; hard? How did you like it? How did you respond to being helped? Is that place your place? How did you feel about your group? What difference did it make that your eyes were closed? What difference did it make after the lights were turned on?

Rationale

The entire exercise can be viewed as an analogy of how we enter a new situation. We enter in "our time" and "alone" and "in the dark." We know little of the objectives, we wander around. Some wander with great hesitancy, others adventurously, still others gropingly. In response to obstacles, some "examine them" and "go around them," a few "push past them," others become hesitant and reluctant to move after being "bumped" a few times, and several may see "being bumped" as a minor irritant to be ignored. Finding a place is easy for some. They are close to a place and take it. For others the process is more difficult. The place they wanted is already occupied, or several people may seek the same place simultaneously, and after a struggle turn and attempt to find another. Still other people find the place they want and will revise the existing structure to include them (bring a chair to a table in which all chairs are occupied). Some people find a place "out of the main-stream," and they are isolated. For a few it is helpful to be guided to a place—to be brought into the mainstream. For others, the "help" means they are put in a position that is not their own. As in life, some will stay, while others, frustrated, will move out. Finally, a few are reluctant to decide on a place—there seems *no place* for them.

Time Required

Depending upon the level of discussion and the number of participants, the exercise will take from 1-2 hours.

2. Initial Membership Experiences—Problem of Belonging to a New Group

Objective

To experience the problems of being in a new group

Setting

The facilitator divides participants into random groups (6-10). A method for doing this may be as follows:

1. "Counting Off"—The facilitator examines the size of the group and determines the number of subgroups needed, based on physical space limitations and an upper limit of 10 in a group. The participants count off 1, 2, 3, 4, 5, 6, 7 (if there are to be, for example, 7 groups). All 1s form one group, 2s the second, etc.
2. "Names in a Hat"—The procedure for ascertaining the number of groups is the same as above, but when the number of groups is determined, slips of paper are placed in a hat or other receptacle. Recipients select a slip. (This is an import-ant method for determining random groups in a large group and especially in an organization. Participants must be very sure that the group in which they are placed is random, or frequently they attribute a variety of other motives for grouping.)
3. "Equalization of Resources"—If the task requires special skills, or participants are made up of departments, groups may be determined as in counting off, but a member of each department is placed in each group to maximize hetero-geneous grouping.

Groups are seated where they can work, and are then assigned a task. For example, they are asked the following questions:
What are the steps in problem solving?
What kind of a leader is most effective in a group?
Can you rank the skills of leadership from most important to least important?
(Skills of leadership should be determined: ability to coordinate, handle disruption, etc. They should be listed, and copies should be made and distributed to each group.)

Action

Groups work on the problem for 15 minutes.

Discussion

The facilitator raises such questions as:
How does it feel to be in a strange group?
What are the problems of new groups?
How efficient do you think your group was?
What would be needed to help it work better in the future?
How did you feel about continuing in the group? (This could be a ranking on a 5-point scale from "would not like to continue" to "would very much like to continue in this group.")

Variation

The exercise is the same as described through the action phase. Following work on the problem, members are given sheets, which they fill in individually and privately. The rating sheet contains the statement: "How would you like to continue working with this group?"

Not at all   Neutral   Definitely
                          (doesn't matter)   yes

(Note that the rating sheet would be marked Time 1.)
The facilitator collects the rating sheets. Then new groups are formed; a member from each of the previous groups forms a new group. They are asked to discuss some of the questions listed in the discussion section. (What are the problems of new groups? How does it feel to be in a strange group? etc.) Following a 15-minute period of working on these questions, a rating sheet like the one previously distri-

buted, but now marked Time 2, is distributed. The procedure for filling out the rating sheets is the same as at Time 1. The sheets are collected. The data from Time 1 and Time 2 are compared. Prior to reporting data, possible discussion questions are:

How was the experience the first time different from the second?
What behaviors were different?
Which group would you have preferred to continue to work in? Why?
Report the results of the data comparisons. Discuss the results.

Comments

This exercise provides the opportunity for a wide range of feelings to be experienced and shared. It can be used as a first experiential learning to acquaint participants with learning from their own experience. It can serve as an example of how data are used to increase the understanding of the process. It can be used to better comprehend that groups must build a common experience to work efficiently—members have to know one another as well as how to work on the task. Finally, it can be used to illustrate that a first meeting will produce norms and a climate that influences how attractive the group is to its members.

3. Conflicts of Multiple Memberships—Alter Ego Exercise[1]

Objectives

To understand the conflicts of multiple memberships and the influences of the various memberships on behavior in a given situation

Setting

The exercise is a role-playing one. Five chairs are placed around a table, and behind each there are two or three others. The chair at the table represents the person; the chairs behind him represent other memberships who speak out to try to influence him. The person then speaks in terms of hearing some influences and ignoring others. Fifteen volunteers are selected. There will be five participants, and two alter egos behind each participant (or more as the situation permits). Participants and alter egos should practice privately and build their cases.

The facilitator should establish a situation for discussion that involves counter influences on a person. An example might be a committee meeting to determine a new high school dress code. Members of the committee could be:

[1] The alter ego technique is discussed in the appendix of the textbook.

President of the Student Body
(Alter Egos)

1. Peer representative—students want a more liberal dress code—jeans, no socks, etc.
2. Football team member—coach thinks athletes should wear hair short; if longer hair passes, it will look more out of place.

Principal of School
(Alter Egos)

1. Faculty representative—students who dress for school more likely to value schooling.
2. Adviser of students—want to be popular; will this reduce effectiveness on other issues?

President of P.T.A.
(Alter Egos)

1. Representative of parents—conservative, would prefer dresses, slacks, not jeans; they are for hay rides or working on lawn; miniskirts indecent.
2. Member of a parents' discussion group—parents must be open to new ideas, not impose their values on children if they don't make sense to children; each generation has its clothing fads—remember yours?

President of Eleventh Grade
Class (Alter Egos)

1. Representative of class—better get a more liberal code—as liberal as possible, or students will think I have done nothing this year, and I won't get re-elected.
2. College aspirant—I need a good recommendation for college from the principal; my scores and grades aren't as good as they might be, and a favorable letter would help. If I antagonize him, it won't be so good.

Faculty Member
(Alter Egos)

1. Faculty member—I'm pretty liberal about what students can wear, but there are some who always want to go further. If you say skirts are allowed 2 inches above the knees, they go 5; if you say button shirts, they wear tee shirts. To preserve any semblance of dress you have to have a more severe code, but enforce it liberally.
2. Parent—kids have so many problems these days—draft, college competition, drugs, authority problems—let them have some feelings of power, of making their own decisions. What difference does it really make what kind of clothes they wear?

Action

The meeting takes place, and the alter egos speak as appropriate. The meeting goes on until a decision is made or it is evident that a decision is impossible.

Discussion

How did multiple memberships affect members' behavior?
Which memberships were influential? Why?
How do multiple memberships influence the productivity of a group? Its efficiency?

Variation

The setting and the action are the same as described previously, except that the facilitator notifies the alter egos that they may not speak the first 5 minutes of the discussion. At the end of the first time period, the alter egos speak to their counterparts and continue to do so for the remainder of the discussion. For this variation, observers can be appointed and asked to note changes in the participants' behavior when there are not alter egos and later when there are.

The participants report their feelings with and without alter egos and tell who they felt influenced their behavior. Reports are then taken from observers, and a discussion as in previous section follows.

4. Reference Groups—Who Am I?

Objectives

To understand people's reference groups
To develop insights that what is a reference group for one person may not be a reference group for another, that reference groups are subjective

Setting

Five chairs are arranged at the front of the room. The facilitator asks for five volunteers and two observers. The volunteers leave the room. The observers are instructed to write down what the volunteers say in response to the question, "Who are you?"

Action

The facilitator calls the volunteers into the room one at a time and asks them to be seated in one of the five chairs. He asks, "Who are you?" He waits for a reply, and then repeats the question. This procedure continues until the facilitator has asked the question 10 times and has received 10 replies. (There should be no comments or additional statements from the facilitator during this period, although he may nod after volunteer's statements to indicate that the volunteer is understanding the question.

The next person is then called in, seated in the next seat, and the previous procedures repeated. This continues until all the volunteers have been questioned.

The observers are asked to write on the board (or newsprint) the names of the volunteers and their replies. (Sometimes this can be expedited by having the same number of observers as volunteers, allowing all the observers to write data simultaneously.)

Discussion

What are the important groups to each person? How do they differ from each other?
What difference will it make since each is a member of a group?

5. *Increasing Attractiveness of the Group—High Status-Low Status*[2]

Attractiveness of a group may be increased by making it better serve the needs of people. A group will be more attractive the more it provides status and recognition.

Objective

To understand that status affects a person's attractiveness to the group; high status has the effect of increasing attractiveness; low status reduces it.

Setting

The facilitator asks for eight volunteers. Four are assigned the role of committee members, four are asked to go outside and await instructions.

A table should be set in the center of the room (or where all can observe) with six chairs. The four committee members will sit at the table. There are two empty chairs for two latecomers. It is agreed in advance that whoever sits in one chair (let us say the red one) will be treated as the superintendent of schools (or the president of the company, or some other high-status position); whoever sits in the other vacant chair will be treated as a new second-grade teacher (or a new production line employee). He is not to be addressed by his title, and no specific reference will be made to his position. A situation is determined as the basis for discussion; for example, a workshop planning committee deciding whether or not to

---

[2]This design is based on an exercise reported by Matthew Miles, in *Learning to work in groups,* New York: Teachers College Press, Columbia University, p. 138.

invite principals to a workshop like this one next year. (Or an industry convention committee deciding whether special efforts should be made to get top management to participate in the convention next year and not just appear on the program.) The facilitator asks the committee members to take a strong position—either for or against. (It is important for them to select the side so that it is understood that one position is not objectively easier or better.)

The facilitator instructs the four people in the hall. He tells the two observers to tally the number of comments directed to the two latecomers by the other group members and, if possible, to write down the nature of the comments made. They return to the room and sit where they can observe the latecomers in the meeting.

The two latecomers are briefed on the question and instructed to take the position opposite to what the others agreed upon (but they are not told it is opposite).

Action

The meeting starts, the two latecomers enter, the observers watch. The role play continues until a decision, or lack of decision, is clear, or until enough behavioral examples are elicited to enable a fruitful discussion.

Discussion

Two latecomers are asked how they liked working with the group. (The high-status person will report that even with a deviant position he was listened to and considered important. The low-status member will report not being listened to or having no influence in the group.) Would they like to continue working with this group? Why? The observers report responses of members to each of the latecomers. They also report the number of times each was addressed and the flavor of comments.

The facilitator then asks the following questions:

When a person is treated as if he has high status, what happens?

How do members behave toward him?

When a person is of low status, how do members behave toward him?

How does he feel toward the group?

Analysis

After the discussion, analysis will show how ideas of high-status people are often accepted without regard to merit, and how feelings of being rejected cause withdrawal, anger, and refusal to present one's good ideas to the group. Using the empty chairs is important to indicate that whoever falls into the accepted or rejected role is a random matter.

6. How Can Attractiveness of a Group Be Increased—The Quiet One Exercise

Some members may want to participate more, but never seem to "get a chance." Others speak first and seem to dominate the discussion. An opportunity to permit the quiet members to participate is likely to increase their feelings of worth and increase the attractiveness of the group for them.

Objectives

To present an opportunity for "the quiet one" to participate
To create greater understanding that being quiet does not mean necessarily that the person has nothing to say
To understand that support influences behavior of a member
To increase insights into possibilities of increasing attractiveness of a group for a member through meeting that member's needs
To permit more active members a role in meeting needs of less active members, in order to develop greater empathy for less active members

Situation

This exercise is used with a group that has been working together previously and where members know each other and are familiar with one another's usual behaviors. The exercise is also appropriate for a number of groups working simultaneously.

The facilitator announces that he will require two members from each group to participate in an exercise. He *selects* (note the deviation from the ask-for-volunteers format) the two most active members of each group and asks them to go outside for briefing.

The facilitator briefs the selected pairs. He asks each representative pair to determine who the most quiet person in their group is. He tells the two pairs to be warm, friendly, supporting, etc. to the target person in the ensuing discussion. He further instructs the two that when they return, one will be chairman of the discussion and the other a participant observer. He asks the observer to be aware of participation by the target person, degree of response to him by other members, and changes in the course of the discussion in regard to target member or relationship of the member to the group.

The two representatives return, and the facilitator announces that in the discussion to follow one of the returnees will be the chairman and the other will be a participant-observer. (No further instructions are given. The members will infer that some phase of leadership, etc. is to be examined.)

Action

The facilitator announces an appropriate subject for discussion, and the discussion continues for 10–15 minutes.

Discussion

Each chairman is asked who the target person was, and the facilitator asks the target person how he felt in the group. Observers and chairmen report on their findings. Others report their feelings with regard to the target person in this situation. Then there is a general discussion on the following questions:

Who finds groups attractive?

How can groups be more attractive to members?

What happens when we stereotype members—when we expect them to act a certain way?

What are the implications for the use of resources of members?

3   exercises in group norms, standards and pressures

Overview of Exercises

1. *Differences between Group Norms (Parsons Model)*   Using data generated within their own groups, participants are faced with the fact that norms not only differ in how they are expressed (explicitly, implicitly, formally, informally) but also stress is created because norms in one group differ dramatically from those in another.
2. *Independence and Submission to Group Pressure*   Using a classic research from social psychology, this activity dramatically reveals how individuals will submit to group pressures and often alter their own viewpoints in order to gain acceptance or because they do not wish to look "stupid" in the eyes of others.
3. *Effects of Group Pressures toward Uniformity*   This exercise helps to focus on the deviant in a group and how he is often censured. The manner in which group pressure is mobilized is particularly evident as patterns of communication shift.

4.   *Group Pressures on Issues*   It has been suggested that decision making is really the process of influencing others to think like ourselves. In this exercise there is pressure on a group to arrive at a group decision. Thus, individuls are faced with either being deviant or bringing their opinions into line with others. How this is done so individuals in most cases save face is one area given attention.

Other Suggested Exercises in the Manual which Relate Directly to the Issue of Group Norms

Chapter 1	Many of the perception and communication exercises depend, to some degree, on previous expectations of group members and the norms they have experienced which now shape their views of reality. Exercises 1, 3, 4, and 6 are particularly useful. Defensive Communication (Norms generated in groups determine the degree individuals are allowed to be open and even what form their defensive behaviors may take.)
Chapter 2	Membership in a group is closely related in many instances to the degree to which individuals are willing to conform to a wide range of group norms. Thus, with a slight shift of focus, Exercises 1, 2, 4, and 5 are quite applicable to the study of norms.
Chapter 4	1. Hidden Agenda Role Play (Norms often determine the degree to which hidden agendas can or cannot be expressed.) 2. Dimensions of Cooperation—Five Squares (This nonverbal exercise generates patterns of expected behaviors very clearly without a word being spoken.)
Chapter 6	5. The Hollow Square 6. The Peg Board Game 18. Maslow's Hierarchy of Needs
Chapter 7	3. The Bag or the Box

1. Differences between Group Norms (Parsons Model)

Objectives

To examine the basis for norms within a group
To examine the differences in norms between two groups
To learn more about norms within a group
To understand more about the effect of norms on group productivity

Setting

The facilitator explains that each group develops its own norms which affect both
the relations among members and the group's productivity. An understanding
of a group's norms will help it examine the appropriateness of its norms and the
areas of stress.
Questionnaires as on page 31 should be distributed.

Action

Members fill in the questionnaires. Members, by groups, analyze the results, and
each group reports back to the entire group. The data may be tabulated as the mean
average reply on the rating scale or it may be on the median reply of persons
responding.

Discussion

The following questions are discussed:
What kind of norms does this group have? On what are the norms based (explicit,
implicit, formal, informal)?
What are the areas of stress?
How appropriate are these norms in terms of the purposes of this group?
Could there be more effective norms? What would they be? How could these norms
be introduced and effectuated?

Variation

This exercise can be a means to contrast two groups with which members are involved. It is effective if one is a small group and the other a secondary organization.
The discussion questions can be the same as above, but there will be an increased
understanding that norms for one group may be inappropriate for another. Yet
another basis from which to examine norms is to use a questionnaire similar to the
one on p. 31, but having respondents answer the question: "In what groups do I
derive the most satisfaction?" Then the four questions are asked. Ensuing discussion
develops understanding that there is not one desirable model; that varying norms
are appropriate in different situations; and that many norms in existing organizations are outmoded.

Reference

Parson, T., Shils, E. A. (Eds.) *Toward a general theory of action.* Cambridge:
Harvard University Press, 1951, pp. 80–88.

QUESTIONNAIRE ON NORMS

1. What are some of the formal rules held by this group which are not followed and for which informal norms have replaced the established rules? (For example, consider time, absenteeism, the use of Robert's Rules, criteria for membership.)

2. Suggest norms that exist around the following areas:
    a. Who speaks and who is listened to (consider the implications of status, age, achievement)?
    b. What kind of language is permissible (slang, swearing, tone of voice, punitive, supportive)?
    c. How are decisions actually made and what unstated norms govern this process (vote, few power people, assuming agreement, rule of discussion)?
    d. How are feelings shown in the group, both in terms of the positive and negative attitudes that may exist?

3. How would you rate this group in the following areas?

    a. Personal Feelings

    ```
    |_____|_____|_____|_____|
    1                2                3                4                5
    Not Expressed                                      Freely Expressed
    ```

    b. Decision Made

    ```
    |_____|_____|_____|_____|
    1                2                3                4                5
    By Individuals                                     Shared
    (in Cliques)
    ```

    c. Acceptance in Group

    ```
    |_____|_____|_____|_____|
    1                2                3                4                5
    Ascribed                                           Achieved
    ```

    d. Achievement in Group

    ```
    |_____|_____|_____|_____|
    1                2                3                4                5
    Personal Qualities                                 Explicit Standards
    (intangibles)                                      (clear criteria)
    ```

2. Independence and Submission to Group Pressure[1]

Purpose

To study independence and submission to group pressure in judgmental tasks concerning a simple, clear matter of fact

To increase the understanding of factors influencing submission in judgments

Method

A five-person group is selected, or there are a number of five-person groups. Each group is told that an experiment in group perception is being conducted. Each member is given his set of instructions and told to follow them; he is not to show his instructions to anyone else.

The participants are seated around a table. Each is given his set of instructions (see pages 33–34). Each member is named (*A–E*). Member *A* (the "naive" subject) should be seated at the end or next to the end of the table. A set of eight cards is made up, as illustrated below.

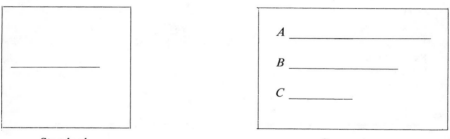

Standard   Comparison

Each member announces his judgment (the standard line is most similar to line *C*, etc.). This is repeated for the eight cards.

Data Analysis

How often does member *A* yield? Under what circumstances? On what level does he yield?

1. Perceptual—subject convinced himself that he saw lines as the majority said (rare—subjects with lack of trust in themselves and unaware they yielded).

[1] This design is based on classic experiments by Solomon Asch, Effects of group pressure upon the modification and distortion of judgments, in H. Gruetzkow (Ed.), *Groups leadership and men*, Pittsburgh, Pa.: Carnegie Press, 1951, pp. 177–190.

2. Judgmental level—subject not sure he understands task or does not want to wreck the experiment (frequent).
3. Action level—occurred in subjects who were very aware of yielding behavior and uncomfortable about it, but they persisted for fear of being excluded, ostracized, or considered eccentric.

Discussion

What are characteristics of conformity?
What motivations might have led to yielding? To independence?

(The following directions are written and handed to the members of each group.)

MEMBER A

This is an experiment in group perception. You will be shown a card with three unequal lines, and you will be asked to match a fourth line to one of them. Then each member will announce his judgment. Your personal instructions are: "You will try to match the lengths of paper to the best of your ability. You will have about two minutes to decide."

MEMBER B

This is an experiment in group perception. You will be shown a card with three unequal lines, and you will be asked to match a fourth line to one of them. Then each member will announce his judgment. Your personal instructions are: "You will purposely choose the wrong one on each card subtly but persistently. You and D must always agree."

MEMBER C

This is an experiment in group perception. You will be shown a card with three unequal lines, and you will be asked to match a fourth line to one of them. Then each member will announce his judgment. Your personal instructions are: "You will agree with the majority on the first two. On the next four you will begin to side with A but at the last minute side with the group. Agree with the group on the last two."

MEMBER D

This is an experiment in group perception. You will be shown a card with three unequal lines, and you will be asked to match a fourth line to one of them. Then each member will announce his judgment. Your personal instructions are: "You will purposely choose the wrong one on each card, but you must always agree with member B."

MEMBER E

This is an experiment in group perception. You will be shown a card with three unequal lines, and you will be asked to match a fourth line to one of them. Then each member will announce his judgment. Your personal instructions are: "You will go along with the majority of the group, but you will try to encourage member D to join the majority opinion."

3. Effects of Group Pressures Toward Uniformity

Objectives

To better understand the process by which groups function to obtain conformity
To provide the basis for examining what group members do to exert influence on one another
To better understand the "deviant's" position
To better understand the dynamics of interventions
To understand the effects of a latecomer

Method[2]

The facilitator groups the participants into clusters of 12–18. He tells each cluster to designate half their group as group *A* and the remainder as group *B*. Group *A* is given sheets 1, 2, and 3 (see pages 35–37) and instructed to scan the materials. Group *B* is given sheet 4 (see page 38). The facilitator asks that they study the observation form, be prepared to observe, and report on their observations. He then asks group *A* to select two of their members to be latecomers to the meeting and instructs the two latecomers, briefing them separately. He gives each a copy of his instructions (see p. 38).

Action

The participants sit around a table; the meeting begins and continues until a unanimous decision has been reached. Then the facilitator sends latecomer 1 in; eight minutes later he sends latecomer 2 into the meeting. (When the latecomers are sent in, he reminds the observers to begin their observations.) The meeting is continued until a high point has been reached, or a decision is reaffirmed or changed. The facilitator then pairs members of group *A* (participants) and members of group *B* (observers) and instructs them to do the following task:

1. Identify how the group's behavior toward each latecomer affected the group's attitude toward its decision.
2. Determine what the group did to influence each latecomer.

---

[2]This design was developed from an experiment by Stanley Schachter in Deviation, rejection, and communication, *Journal of Abnormal and Social Psychology*, 1951, *46*, 190–207.

SHEET 1 – THE SITUATION

You are citizens of a community in which a new superintendent of schools has just been hired. The superintendent is eager to obtain some knowledge of your attitudes concerning the proper treatment of children who get into trouble in the schools and in the community.

The superintendent has asked you to discuss what you would want him to do with a typical case. His interest is not in the specific method of treatment, but rather in your attitudes toward children who are in trouble. You have been invited to meet in the living room of a member of the group.

The superintendent has decided it would be wise for him not to be present at the meeting. He has furnished you with two documents: one document is a brief summary of the case on which he wants your counsel, the other is a scale he calls a "love-punishment scale." He has asked you to arrive at a unanimous decision concerning the point on this scale which best expresses your opinion.

You are informed upon arrival that two persons are late and will be coming in soon. You are not to wait for them but are to proceed with making your decision.

SHEET 2- REGIONAL CITY PUBLIC SCHOOLS

Summary of Case No. 217   Name: Johnny Rocco

Johnny is the third child in an Italian family of seven children. He says that he has not seen his father for several years. His only recollection of his father is that he used to come home drunk and would beat every member of the family. Everyone ran when Father came staggering home. Mother, according to Johnny, has not been much better. She is constantly irritable and unhappy. She has always told Johnny that he would come to no good end. She has had to work, when her health allowed her to do so, and has been so busy keeping the family supplied with food and clothing that she has had little time to be the kind of mother she would like to be.

Johnny began to skip school when in the seventh grade. He is now in the ninth grade and is having great difficulty in conforming to the school routine. He seldom has lessons prepared, often misbehaves in class, is frequently a truant, and has been in a number of fights with schoolmates in the past year.

Two years ago he was caught stealing from a local variety store. Since that time, he has been picked up by police for stealing, for destroying property, and for being on the streets at a very late hour. Police have spotted him as a "bad one."

The court dealt with the matter by appointing a "big brother" to care for Johnny. The man, Mr. O'Brien, has brought the first semblance of discipline into Johnny's life. Through Mr. O'Brien, Johnny got a job running errands in a grocery store. Thus far, he has worked well on the job, although he complains that his boss is too strict.

One teacher has great appeal for Johnny. She teaches English. He says that she is the only kind and thoughtful person he has known and that he would do anything for her. Despite this statement, Johnny has not shown good work in her classes. He apparently spends most of his time in English class in some sort of daydream. The teacher has had very little contact with Johnny outside of her class

Next year Johnny will be in senior high school. This will enable the school system to make counseling services available for him. The schools do not provide professional help for students in junior high school or below. The school principal has been attempting to deal with Johnny for the past 2 years.

In the senior high school, a number of things may be done, or arranged, for Johnny. A well-organized program of study fitted to Johnny's abilities and interests can be developed. It is also possible to have Johnny put into a foster home, through the help of the State Children's Institute, or to have him committed to the State Vocational School for Boys.

What plan the school system will follow next year depends, of course, on how Johnny behaves in the next few months. In general, the schools want to follow policies that are acceptable to the citizens of the community.

SHEET 3– LOVE-PUNISHMENT SCALE

It is important to note that Johnny is not an attractive child, and he is weak, sickly, and shows signs of malnutrition. What kind of attention should the public schools try to arrange for Johnny?

1. Give Johnny very much love, warmth, and affection so that he learns that he can depend on others and that they will protect him and overlook his misbehavior.
2. Give Johnny understanding treatment of both his personal and his family difficulties, based on careful diagnosis, so that Johnny can learn to handle his problems with the help of others when he needs it.
3. Help Johnny's mother set up a more wholesome family life.
4. Give Johnny impersonal attention in an orderly routine so that he can learn to stand on his own feet.
5. Give Johnny a well-structured schedule of daily activities with immediate and unpleasant consequences for breaking rules.
6. Provide strict control over Johnny's activities and immediate attention to misbehavior, so that he will learn adult standards for behavior.
7. Create very strict and very strong controls over every event in Johnny's daily life together with immediate and strong punishment for misbehavior.

SHEET 4- OBSERVATION INSTRUMENT

Instructions: 1. Keep a tally of the number of times comments are made to each latecomer.
2. Jot down the nature of the comments as much as possible.
3. Make notes on what members of the group *do* to the latecomers.

Latecomer One Tally of number of comments		*Latecomer Two* Tally of number of comments	
Nature of comments	What members of group did	Nature of comments	What members of group did

LATECOMER ONE

You believe that point 6 on the scale (sheet 3) best expresses your opinion. When you arrive at the meeting, please stick to this opinion.

You like this group very much; you like the topic under discussion. You are proud to have been asked to attend the meeting and think you will get a lot out of it. Many of your friends admire your activity in this advisory group.

LATECOMER TWO

You believe that point 6 on the scale (sheet 3) best expresses your opinion. When you arrive at the meeting, please stick to this opinion.

You dislike this group very much; you don't like the topic. You are sure that this discussion will be a waste of time and that your friends would laugh at your spending time discussing this topic.

3. On newsprint, write three learnings you derived from the exercise, and share them with the rest of the group.

The pairs post their newsprint reports on the wall.

Discussion

How does pressure to conform affect interpersonal relations?
How does pressure to conform affect the group task?
What are the relationships?

Other Possible Areas for Discussion Can Include the Following:

1. A group that has formed a mutually agreeable decision tries to protect its decision (in this case it was their own property reached by joint discussion).
2. A person whose beliefs deviate from this opinion is put under pressure to conform.
3. Most of the communications are directed toward the deviant.
4. If members perceive that they are making the latecomer uncomfortable, they may try to adjust communications so that no difference of opinion is seen to exist; thus there is no deviant.
5. The deviant under pressure is often quite uncomfortable.
6. It is easier to resist the group pressures when one is not attracted to a group than when one is highly attracted to the group.

4. Group Pressures on Issues

Objectives

To understand how group pressure affects an individual
To illustrate the influence of group decision making
To learn the distinction between individual responses and individual responses after consensus or discussion

Design

The facilitator distributes the questionnaire on page 40 to each of the participants. He requests that the participants fill in the answers as honestly as possible; the questionnaires may be answered anonymously. After the questionnaires are collected, the participants are divided into small groups (6–10). The facilitator distributes additional copies of the questionnaire to each participant as well as an addi-

---

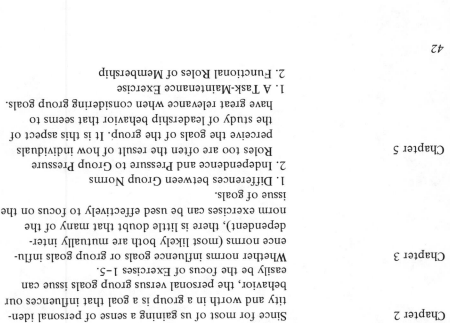

4 exercises in group goals

Overview of Exercises

1. *Hidden Agenda Role Play* Most of us spend a great deal of energy trying to subtly (or not so subtly) influence the decisions being made so that they meet our own needs. Often this is done in a manner that is hidden from the group. This exercise explores the importance of that phenomenon to the group as a whole and the need to raise such issues to the surface.

2. *Dimensions of Cooperation—Five Squares* This activity reveals the degree to which individual goals and group goals often conflict and how groups will differ in their effectiveness depending on the degree to which group goals can be determined and followed.

Other Suggested Exercises in the Manual which Relate Directly to the Issues Surrounding Group Goals

Chapter 1 Personal needs (which determine many of our personal goals and perceptions) are raised in Exercises 1–8.
10. The Observation of Nonverbal Behavior in a Group

Chapter 2 The design of this exercise (simulation used) clearly raises the issue of personal versus group goals in terms of both past expectations and present needs.
Since for most of us gaining a sense of personal identity and worth in a group is a goal that influences our behavior, the personal versus group goals issue can easily be the focus of Exercises 1–5.

Chapter 3 Whether norms influence goals or group goals influence norms (most likely both are mutually interdependent), there is little doubt that many of the norm exercises can be used effectively to focus on the issue of goals.
1. Differences between Group Norms
2. Independence and Pressure to Group Pressure

Chapter 5 Roles too are often the result of how individuals perceive the goals of the group. It is this aspect of the study of leadership behavior that seems to have great relevance when considering group goals.
1. A Task-Maintenance Exercise
2. Functional Roles of Membership

tional one to record the group answer. He asks the p... question by groups and to arrive at a *single decision* on each of the quest... decision which represents their group's feelings on the subject. A discussion follows, and the summary sheets are collected. Each group should be named at the top of the sheet. Each person answers his questionnaire as an individual. (If possible, this might be done after a break or at a later session.) The questionnaire may be responded to anonymously, but the group name appears at the top.

The facilitator tabulates the replies to the first questionnaire (the individual replies) and records (on a blackboard or newsprint) the group decisions on each of the questions. He tabulates and records the replies to the individual questionnaires following the group decisions and indicates the individual replies under the group answer.

Discussion

1. How are replies the first time different from the second individual replies?
2. How do groups influence individuals? What implications?
3. Do people act differently in a group than they act as individuals? How? What difference does it make?
4. How does group discussion influence individual judgments? Are there implications for social change?
   Was there a difference in degree of group replies on the first two questions, as opposed to third and fourth questions? (The first two were concerned with personal choices, the second two with social issues). How were final individual replies influenced by the group on the first two questions, on the last two questions?

QUESTIONNAIRE

The following issues generate a great deal of discussion. How do you feel about each of these issues? Circle the answer you consider most representative of how you feel.

1. Would you marry someone of a different religion?
Definitely
Probably
Undecided
Probably not
Definitely not

2. Would you marry someone of a different race?
Definitely
Probably
Undecided
Probably not
Definitely not

3. Should abortion be legalized?
Definitely
Probably
Undecided
Probably not
Definitely not

4. Should marijuana be legalized?
Definitely
Probably
Undecided
Probably not
Definitely not

Chapter 6

Goals must be considered integrally as part of the problem-solving process. Thus, again, it is relatively easy to adapt many of the problem-solving activities to the issues surrounding goals.

See activities for Viewing the Problem-solving Process (personal versus group goals and their influence on perception and eventual decisions reached)
5. The Hollow Square (focus on goals at various levels of an organization)
7. The Nonzero Sum Game (how trust or distrust can influence the goals of a group)
12. The Devil's Dilemma (a practical means of clarifying goals in terms of their appropriateness)
17. The Process Diagnosis

1. Hidden Agenda Role Play

Objectives

To increase the understanding that groups work simultaneously at an explicit as well as an implicit or hidden level
To increase learnings about "hidden agendas"

Rationale

Each of us has all of the personal, private needs that motivate our behavior in addition to the publicly stated reasons for our being present in a group. We all operate from these hidden agendas to some extent; they are part of us. The issue is not to label them bad, or to ignore them, but to be aware of them in our efforts to understand what is happening in a group. The role play presented allows members to understand the hidden agendas and to become aware that in making sense out of the meeting, these implicit goals greatly influence movement on the group goals.

Design

The facilitator asks for four volunteers to participate in a role play. The volunteers are selected, and each is given a piece of paper with the role he is to play. The role players are given a few minutes to study their roles and be sure they understand them.

The roles on the pieces of paper are as follows:

1. Not only are you very anxious to be elected to this committee but you seriously

believe that unless you are the one elected, it might not be successful. You like your fellow faculty members, but you feel that they tend to be authoritarian, and you are afraid if anyone else is elected, the students will be allowed to make decisions in name, but they will not be allowed to really influence the decisions. You feel very strongly that young people should learn autonomy and responsibility.

2.   You are anxious to be elected. You are taking courses for your doctorate. You want to become a principal. The activity will look good on your record. It might even develop into a vice-principalship in this school.

3.   Not only are you very anxious to be elected to the committee, you seriously believe that unless you are the one elected, the committee might not be successful. You like and respect your fellow faculty members as teachers, but you seriously believe that they do not understand the sort of guidance that students (who are really still children) need in order to learn how to behave responsibly on committees. You feel that if you are elected to this committee, you can guide these students to success, and this will then make a student-faculty disciplinary committee a permanent thing. You are afraid if the other faculty members get the job, the whole thing will result in chaos, and the whole movement will be dropped.

4.   You are in a hurry to leave the meeting, but the principal has asked that you be on the committee, and you want to stay on his good side. You had a fight with someone you are considering marrying last night. You are anxious for the meeting to end so that you can meet her.

Aside from the four role players, the others are asked to be observers for the role play. They are asked to note:
How clear is the goal?
Is it understandable?
Is it attainable?
Are the steps to goal accomplishment known?
How productive is the group?
What impedes the members?
At this point the role players are asked to be seated at a table.

Action

The committee is told that they are members of a high school faculty. The students have asked for more responsibility in determining matters of discipline. The principal has agreed to the establishment of a committee to handle such matters. The membership will be made up of students with one faculty adviser also serving on the committee.

The principal feels that each of the members he has invited would be a suitable faculty adviser. He hopes the faculty committee will determine among themselves whom they would like to represent them. The committee is meeting after school.

The members will decide who the faculty adviser will be and submit his name to the principal so that he can announce it at the assembly in the morning.

The committee meets. The facilitator should break in after about 5–7 minutes if no decision is made, and the role play should be cut so that interest does not wane.

Discussion

Observers are asked to report what they saw.
If the group goal was clear, why was progress so slow? In many groups this role play is not resolved; there is no decision made. If all the members understand the goal, and it is attainable, and the members know the steps to attain it, why is the group not more productive? What impeded the group from arriving at a simple decision? Consider the roles. Who wanted the job? Why?
What were the members' hidden agendas? (What seemed to be motivating them?)
How do private goals (hidden agendas) influence group goals and productivity?
What are the implications for other groups?

2. Dimensions of Cooperation—Five Squares[1]

Objectives

To experience some of the aspects of cooperation
To have data for evaluating one's own behavior in a cooperative situation
To become aware of behaviors which help and hinder group problem solving
To become more sensitive to others in the group in order to be more helpful

Rationale

All of us are quite sure we are cooperative, sensitive, open to others, and willing to be helpful; it comes as a surprise and a powerful learning experience to see ourselves withholding resources, being sensitive only to some people, or being smug. This exercise involves putting together pieces of cardboard in what seems like a game but it generates styles of behavior typical of the participants in other interpersonal relations. The exercise is especially effective because even if participants are reluctant to express openly and to share their learnings about themselves, they are newly aware of their own behavior. They develop a new respect and understanding for the difficulties, frustrations, and rewards of a cooperative working relationship.

[1] This design is based on Communication patterns in task-oriented groups by Alex Bevalos; in D. Cartwright and A. Zander, *Group dynamics: research and theory,* New York: Harper and Row, 1968, p. 510.

Materials

One set of five envelopes is given to each group. Groups will consist of 6–7 members, depending upon whether each group has one or two observers. (See instructions (p. 49), for making up the squares and placing them in the envelopes.)

Overall Objectives

Participants are given envelopes with pieces of cardboard inside. In a nonverbal exercise, people may give their pieces to others and receive pieces. The object of the game is that each person has before him a completed, approximately 6-inch square.

Design

The facilitator divides the participants into random groups of 6–7 members. He asks that one (or two) be designated as observers. The observers go to one corner of the room and are instructed by the facilitator. The observers are instructed to: notice who shares first, who completes the first square and what happens, whether there is a leadership pattern, whether all share the work or it is dumped on one person, and especially note members who give up their pieces and are not given any in return. This might be written and distributed to the observers. At the same time each observer is given a packet of five envelopes and asked to give them to each of the members of his group when so instructed. The observers return to their groups. The facilitator then announces the exercise as an experience they will enjoy and gives the instructions that follow.

He should practice reading the instructions privately, so that he can do it clearly, perhaps with some illustrations as, "You may not ask for a piece verbally or nonverbally. You cannot say, 'John, hand me the large triangle,' nor can you say it in sign language or communicate in a way that asks for a piece."

At this point questions are directed for the sake of clarification. Groups should be reminded that they are to follow the instructions and that each group has an observer to see to it that the rules are followed. The observers should be reminded to note how groups follow rules. Observers distribute one envelope to each participant. The groups are instructed to begin. When a group has completed the problem and each member has a square in front of him, the members should raise their hands. How long it has taken the group to complete the task is noted on the board. (This increases competition within and among groups.)

The time to complete the exercise varies. Some groups will finish in a few minutes, others may take as long as 40 minutes. As a group finishes, the facilitator checks that there is a square before each member, and asks that all the pieces marked *a* be put in the *A* envelope, the *b* pieces in the *B* envelope, etc. so that the set is ready for the next use. (Players do not mind, and the sorting would be a time-consuming task for the facilitator.) He tells the finished group to be aware of their feelings because they will have an opportunity to discuss what happened. Then he tells them that they may observe any other group but they may not speak or in any way interfere with the actions of that group. This has the dual effect of heightening the tensions for remaining groups and enhancing the competitive aspect even within a cooperative situation. In addition, members who were not aware of some of the kinds of behavior exhibited in their own group can see it rather easily when watching another.

As groups finish, the facilitator gives each the same instructions.

The question of what to do when some groups do not finish for a long period is a difficult one. Sometimes the group is blocked because some members have a wrong square and are smugly sitting with it, leaving one person with a few pieces. The facilitator might take one of the pieces from the completed square and give it to the struggling remaining person. This usually gets everyone reinvolved in the problem. Sometimes one person has the correct pieces but cannot see the way to arrange them. One intervention here is to ask someone who seems bursting to put it together what he could do to help, knowing that he may not manipulate another person or his pieces. He frequently slides his completed square to the person and in return receives the ill-matched pieces. In interventions it is important that they not be considered until most of the group have completed their squares, and then only because someone is blocked. If they are continuing to work, they should be left alone. If they are blocked, the facilitator makes a minimum number of interventions, usually only one, which helps the group see another aspect of the problem and helps them renew their efforts toward a solution.

The time each group finishes can be posted on the board. In the following discussion it becomes a strong point to bring to the group's attention that with a problem of the same difficulty and with the same numerical resources, some groups take seven and ten times as long as others to complete the problem.

Discussion

Observers feed back their findings to the group. Members share how they felt.

In the group discussion there is usually a great deal of involvement, and the discussion is quite lively. There may simply be a sharing of feelings through various stages of the problem. Another procedure is to distribute Questions to Guide Individual Reflection (see page 50). Members are asked to answer these questions individually in terms of their feelings and observations. Then groups share their reflections. Finally the total group reports which behaviors they found helped and which hindered, and members determine what generalizations can be made.

Yet another approach is to use the questions from the Guide as the basis for addressing questions to the group for a general session.

Still another approach is to recap the entire sequence of events, and to permit members to discuss their feelings. For example, we start and hope we can "go it" alone. We first try to form our square. As we begin to see others, we notice the situation is unfair. Some people have two pieces, some three, some four. For the philosophers, there is the analogy to each of us coming into life with our own unique resources. It seems that some of us have more and some less, but each is a unique combination. When a member begins to give of his pieces (his resources), what does this encourage in others? They, too, share. The next significant event is that someone gets a square. How does that person feel? Typically he feels self-satisfied and as if he has solved the problem. He finds it difficult to break up his piece. The analogy once more is that we find it difficult to break up what seems to be a correct answer, perhaps what we believe is the only possible answer.

The facilitator continues in this manner discussing leadership patterns, taking of responsibility, noticing how people felt when they were excluded, to whom people were sensitive and to whom not, how the group changed over time, etc. With this last question, most groups report that initially they would give away pieces they did not need. Over time, they became sensitive to the others and attempted to give them what *they* needed.

Variations

This exercise may be used to develop an increased understanding of the concept of cooperation. The group of six is instructed to divide into two's. They are asked to think about cooperation and come up with a definition. Then ideas are shared with the others at the table, and they are instructed to formulate a definition by the entire group (six). They are also asked to list some of the behaviors that aid in cooperation. A report is given, and two lists are made, one on newsprint of combined definitions and on another sheet a list of cooperative behaviors. Then the facilitator says that this will be tested in an exercise, and he proceeds with the instructions listed previously under Design.

With groups that have difficulties communicating or working, this increases awareness of behaviors of "in and out" groups and greatly enhances a more honest communication. Pairs are matched by opposites (blacks-whites, parents-teenagers, men-women), and asked to get to know one another. Each person describes how he feels it must be like to be the other. A white talks about how he thinks it would feel to be the black person opposite him. Then they reverse. This takes about 15 minutes. Then the three groups join and talk to one another. After a few minutes they share how it felt telling the other person what it was like to be that person, how accurate he was, how much was stereotyped. Usually, this initial exchange is strained. There is little trust; each partner is guarded and careful not to reveal much. The conversation is polite and frequently drags.

The facilitator then has the groups do the exercise, and the entire climate of the relationship becomes more honest. Members become aware that they were more sensitive to their own needs than to the needs of others, and more sensitive to their group than the other group. They become annoyed when the first person to get a square is from the other group; it destroys a stereotype that they are better. Over time there is a feeling of bond, of working together, of a genuine relationship. A discussion afterward on differences, similarities, stereotypes, and helping relationships becomes very meaningful.

INSTRUCTIONS TO THE GROUP

In this package are five envelopes, each of which contains pieces of cardboard for forming squares. When the facilitator gives the signal to begin, the task of your group is to form five squares of equal size. The task will not be completed until each individual has before him a perfect square of the same size as that held by others.

Specific limitations are imposed on your group during this exercise:

1. No member may speak.
2. No member may ask another member for a card or in any way signal that another person is to give him a card.
3. Members may, however, give cards to other members.

Are the instructions clear? (Questions are answered.)
The facilitator gives the signal to begin working.

DIRECTIONS FOR MAKING A SET OF SQUARES

There is a set of five envelopes containing pieces of cardboard which have been cut in different patterns and which when properly arranged will form five squares of equal size. One set should be provided for each group of five persons. Since groups often run from 15 to 20 persons, it is suggested that the facilitator make four sets.

To prepare a set, cut out five cardboard squares of equal size, approximately six by six inches. Place the squares in a row and mark them as below, penciling the letters, *a, b, c,* etc. lightly so that they can be erased.

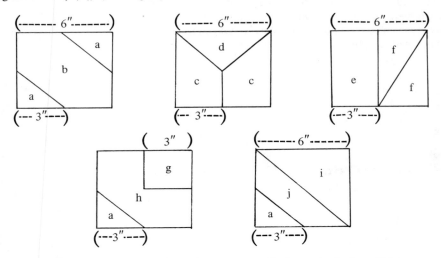

The lines should be so drawn that when cut out, all pieces marked *a* will be of exactly the same size, all pieces marked *c* of the same size, etc. By using multiples of 3 inches, several combinations will be possible that enable participants to form one or two squares, but only one combination is possible that will form five of them six by six inches.

After drawing the lines on the six-by-six-inch squares and labeling them with lower-case letters, cut each square as marked into smaller pieces to make the parts of the puzzle. Mark each of five envelopes, *A, B, C, D,* and *E*. Distribute the cardboard pieces in the five envelopes as follows:

Envelope *A:*   *i, h, e*
       B: *a, a, a, c*
       C: *a, j*
       D: *d, f*
       E: *g, b, f, c*

Erase the penciled letter from each piece and write, instead, the appropriate envelope letter, as envelope *A*, etc. This will make it easy to return the pieces to the proper envelope for subsequent use when a group has completed the task.

QUESTIONS TO GUIDE INDIVIDUAL REFLECTION

1. When someone holding a key piece did not see the solution:
   What do you think other members felt?
   What clues did you pick up that made you think so?
2. When someone had completed his square incorrectly and then sat back with a self-satisfied smile on his face:
   What would you guess were his feelings?
   What reactions did you notice from other members?
   What would you *guess* they were feeling?
   What were your own feelings?
3. When a person could not see the solution as quickly as others:
   What did you think was the feeling of the others toward him?
   What were your own feelings toward him?
4. What evidence did you see of trying to help another?
5. What evidence did you see of trying to get him out of the group?

5 exercises in leadership

Overview of Exercises

1. *A Task-Maintenance Exercise* This role-play activity helps the participants to view the differences that exist between task and maintenance roles in a group. Specific behaviors are noted and their value explored. By studying such behaviors it is possible to alter patterns of behavior established in decision-making groups.

2. *Functional Roles of Membership* This activity provides another avenue for exploring many of the issues raised in the first exercise. In this case, participants are provided a specific task to generate a variety of leadership requirements. How well the group is able to use its own resources in meeting these particular needs provides a useful basis for the discussion of functional roles.

3. *Increasing Understanding of Leadership and Power* This series of five exercises focuses on a variety of issues that are usually raised when exploring leadership issues. Thus, the multiple role concept of leadership is viewed in exercise 3a—How Many Leaders? The dimensions of power in the group are played out in exercise 3b, and a discussion of types of leadership can easily be generated. Other personal issues relating to participant status in the group (3c), personal identity in the group (3d), and fantasies of influence (3e), are the focus of the other exercises.

4. *Power Questionnaire* By exploring the internal dynamics of power within their own group(s) the participants provide data that will help them understand the dimensions of power in groups and the degree to which certain aspects of power tend to predominate in a group.

5. *64 Squares—Different Leadership Styles* Findings from a classic study in social psychology are explored by comparing data gathered in a similar group experiment involving the participants. The aim is to help clarify the advantages and disadvantages of various leadership styles and their implications for those involved. (Autocratic, laissez-faire, and democratic styles of leadership are explored.)

6. *Decision Making along a Continuum—Problems* Leadership is explored by means of viewing a variety of situations requiring multilateral versus unilateral decisions and active versus more passive leadership styles. The exercise produces considerable conflict which may raise other interpersonal issues. There should be enough time allocated to deal with all of the issues that are generated from the design.

7. *Leadership Questionnaire* A questionnaire provides a low-threat vehicle for discussing the leadership issues that are important to various participants. Each individual is requested to view leadership from his own perspective. Leadership expectations are drawn from the group and explored in relation to issues of membership, norms, and goals.

Other Suggested Exercises in the Manual Which Relate Directly to Issues Surrounding Leadership In most cases, the best way to learn about leadership, once it has been clearly defined, is by watching people in the process of influencing one another. Successful and unsuccessful leadership attempts as well as various leadership styles can be explored in the following exercises.

Chapter 1 6. The Old Lady–Young Lady
9. The Group Dynamics Tango (leadership issues between individuals)
12. The Perception of Other Group Members—An Initial View

Chapter 2 5. Increasing Attractiveness of the Group—High

1. A Task-Maintenance Exercise

Objectives

To increase understanding of task-maintenance roles
To increase skills in observing a group; to learn to categorize by functional roles of members
To increase learnings about the difference between intended behavior and perceived behavior

Rationale

This exercise permits participants and observers to understand that intent is not enough. Attempting certain behaviors does not mean that a person will be perceived in the role he intends. In addition, intending to behave in a certain way does not indicate a person's skill in this role, factors that may interfere with his intentions, or the fact that more conscious behaviors are called into play. Participants come to understand some of the complexities in the interpersonal and group processes that go on in meetings.

This exercise is not appropriate unless the members have become familiar with the task-maintenance concept and functional roles and are willing to consider the implications of the learnings. It can be followed by skill sessions in practicing each of the task and maintenance roles. The role play may be repeated after discussion, or skill session, with members attempting to be more congruent or skillful in their roles, and observers attempting to focus more clearly on behaviors.

Materials

The following materials are needed: two copies of the role-play situation described below and six role-play names; six copies of the Explanation Sheet of Task and Maintenance Roles (see p. 55), which are to be given to role players only; Observer Forms (Task Functions and Maintenance Functions) for all members of the group (see pp. 56–57); newsprint, magic markers, and tape; and a table and six chairs for the role play.

Design

The facilitator introduces the design as a role play. He explains that in a role play a situation is concocted that is not real but could be. Participants do not enact their usual roles but rather the roles that they are instructed to play. The role play permits an examination of behavior without embarrassing anyone and helps develop increased skills in the situation.

The facilitator asks for six volunteers to participate in the role play. He selects six people and briefs them in private. He distributes six pieces of paper (usually face down, and the role players select one of the papers). The papers should read as follows:

Association President—assume number 1 task role and number 1 maintenance role.
Teacher Representative—assume number 2 task role and number 2 maintenance behavior.
Association Negotiator—assume number 3 task role and number 3 maintenance role.
Superintendent of Schools—assume number 4 task role and number 4 maintenance role.
School Board Representative—assume number 5 task role and number 5 maintenance role.
School Board President—assume number 6 task role and number 6 maintenance role. You are somewhat hostile to the teachers and their position on the salary increase.

The association negotiators, the board, and the superintendent are given a few minutes to discuss as individual groups what they plan to do. While they are doing this, observer sheets are distributed to others in the group.

The facilitator instructs observers to tally every time any of the role players behave either under Task or Maintenance. He asks them to record words or acts that will help recall and support their observations and also to write the names of the role players at the top of the sheets. The facilitator answers any questions observers may have. Then he calls the role players back into room, seats them at the conference table, and reads the role play to the entire group. He gives one copy to the role players to keep before them.

The Role-Play Situation

A negotiations impasse over salaries between the Teachers Association and the school board is imminent. The association's original proposal called for a beginning salary of $7,600 with a $200-a-year increment for 12 years. This would have given the association the highest beginning and ending salary in the country.

The first counterproposal by the board maintains the existing salary of $7,600, but with $100 per year increments for 12 years. This was refused by the association. A second counterproposal by the board maintains the existing salary increment of $200 per year for 20 years, but begins at $6,400. This would give the association the lowest starting salary in the country but the highest maximum salary. A special levy has already been called for, and the amount, which includes no salary adjustment, has been earmarked. As the scene opens, the board members say that they cannot change the earmarking of the special levy funds and that no other funds are available. The teachers say that they cannot accept the last proposal, maintaining that it will decimate the professional staff of the district. The association negotiators have agreed that if they cannot get the board to utilize the reserve funds (7½ percent of the total budget), they will declare an impasse at the present meeting.

The facilitator continues the role-play situation for 10–15 minutes. He cuts it when it appears that there will be no further movement, before interest lags. Then he asks observers to meet in trios and compare their perceptions and tallying. The trios do this and arrive at a joint report indicating what role each player was primarily playing (about 10 minutes). The facilitator returns to the general session and places the names of role players on newsprint. He asks for reports from trios, and next to each name he writes the role the trio thought each person was taking. Then he asks each role player to reveal the role assigned to him and what he was attempting. That information is written next to his name on the newsprint. The prediction is that there will be a discrepancy between the way the role player understood his role and the way he actually acted it out. Also, it is predictable that the observers will vary in their reports of how the role players were acting.

Discussion

Role players are asked how comfortable they were in their roles. Was it like their usual roles?
Which players enacted their roles most faithfully—were they perceived by others as being in their assigned roles? Which players had the greatest discrepancies? Why? Which behaviors caused difficulties in attempting to attain observer agreement? Are there generalizations that can be made about our observations?

The facilitator might briefly dwell on the several factors that influence the interpersonal and group processes going on at meetings. At least two factors appear prominent as a result of this role play:
1. *A perceptual factor.* Not all of us perceive the same thing when we are watch-

EXPLANATION SHEET OF TASK AND MAINTENANCE ROLES[1]
(To be given to role players only)

Task Roles

1. *Initiating*: Proposing tasks or goals: defining a group problem; suggesting a procedure or ideas for solving a problem.

2. *Information or opinion seeking*: Requesting facts; seeking relevant information about a group concern; asking for suggestions and ideas.

3. *Information or opinion giving*: Offering facts; providing relevant information about group concern stating a belief; giving suggestions or ideas.

4. *Clarifying or elaborating*: Interpreting or reflecting ideas and suggestions; clearing up confusion; indicating alternatives and issues before the group; giving examples.

5. *Summarizing*: Pulling together related ideas; restating suggestions after the group has discussed them; offering a decision or conclusion for the group to accept or reject.

6. *Consensus testing*: Sending up trial balloons to see if group is nearing a conclusion; checking with group to see how much agreement has been reached.

Maintenance Roles

1. *Encouraging*: Being friendly, warm, and responsive to others; accepting others and their contributions; regarding others by giving them an opportunity or recognition.

2. *Expressing group feelings*: Sensing feelings, mood, relationships within the group; sharing his own feelings or affect with other members.

3. *Harmonizing:* Attempting to reconcile disagreements; reducing tension through "pouring oil on troubled waters"; getting people to explore their differences.

4. *Compromising*: When his own idea or status is involved in a conflict, offering to compromise his own position; admitting error, disciplining himself to maintain group cohesion.

5. *Gate-keeping*: Attempting to keep communication channels open; facilitating the participation of others; suggesting procedures for sharing opportunity to discuss group problems.

6. *Setting standards*: Expressing standards for the group to achieve; applying standards in evaluating group functioning and production.

[1] (Based on Benne and Sheats, 1948)

TASK FUNCTIONS– OBSERVER FORM

Names								
1. *Initiating*: Proposing tasks or goals; defining a group problem; suggesting a procedure or ideas for solving a problem.								
2. *Information or opinion seeking*: Requesting facts; seeking relevant information about a group concern; asking for suggestions or ideas.								
3. *Information or opinion giving*: Offering facts; providing relevant information about group concern; stating a belief; giving suggestions or ideas.								
4. *Clarifying or elaborating*: Interpreting or reflecting ideas and suggestions; clearing up confusion; indicating alternatives and issues before the group; giving examples.								
5. *Summarizing*: Pulling together related ideas; restating suggestions after group has discussed them; offering a decision or conclusion for the group to accept or reject.								
6. *Consensus testing*: Sending up trial balloons to see if the group is nearing a conclusion; checking with the group to see how much agreement has been reached.								

MAINTENANCE FUNCTIONS- OBSERVER FORM

Names							
1. *Encouraging*: Being friendly, warm and responsive to others; accepting others and their contributions; regarding others by giving them an opportunity or recognition.							
2. *Expressing group feelings*: Sensing feelings, mood, relationships within the group; sharing his own feeling or affect with other members.							
3. *Harmonizing*: Attempting to reconcile disagreements; reducing tension through "pouring oil on troubled waters"; getting people to explore their differences.							
4. *Compromising*: When his own idea or status is involved in a conflict, offering to compromise his own position; admitting error, disciplining himself to maintain group cohesion.							
5. *Gate-keeping*: Attempting to keep communication channels open; facilitating the participation of others; suggesting procedures for sharing opportunity to discuss group problems.							
6. *Setting standards*: Expressing standards for the group to achieve; applying standards in evaluating group function and production.							

ing the behavior of another person. Some perceive a person giving feelings, while others hear him giving information or expressing opinions.

2. *Our intentions are different from our behavior.*   Participants might have intended to play a given role but might have given out mixed messages. Their words said one thing, but their nonverbal behavior in body or tone emitted another message.

Sometimes we intend to play roles at which we are not skilled; we mean to behave in a certain way but get "off the track." Sometimes cues from another person evoke responses we had not intended. We sense that he does not like us, and we become defensive or see him as an opponent when we previously assumed he was a friend. How we feel about others personally affects our behavior.

2. Functional Roles of Membership

Objectives

To increase the understanding of functional roles of membership
To see leadership emerge
To practice observing types of behavior
To develop an increased understanding of leadership requiring followership

Materials

The materials needed are the same as for the role play or tower exercise, enough for all participants. Also needed are copies of Group Building and Maintenance Roles (see p. 59) and Group Task Roles (see p. 60).

Rationale

Any of the role-play exercises in the book or problem-solving exercises in this chapter are appropriate as a situation to examine functional roles of members. The goal is to develop skills in observing types of behavior and increasing awareness of the functional roles.

Design

The facilitator establishes the role-play or problem-solving exercise (see p. 61), or uses tinker toys and asks each group to create a symbol of its group. Or he can use newsprint, crayons, and other materials and ask each group to create a collage for their group. Two observers are assigned to tally for functional roles. Each time someone behaves in a role a tally is made. One person can tally for task roles, the

GROUP BUILDING AND MAINTENANCE ROLES

Categories describing the types of member behavior required for building and maintaining the group as a working unit.

Usually helpful	*Usually destructive*
1. *Encouraging*: Being friendly, warm and responsive to others; accepting others and their contributions; giving to others.	Being cold, unresponsive, unfriendly; rejecting others' contributions; ignoring them.
2. *Expressing feelings*: Expressing feelings present in the group; calling attention of the group to its reactions to ideas and suggestions; expressing his own feelings or reactions in the group.	Ignores reactions of the group as a whole, refuses to express his own feelings when needed.
3. *Harmonizing*: Attempts to reconcile disagreements; reduces tension through joking, relaxing comments; gets people to explore their differences.	Irritates or "needles" others; encourages disagreement for its own sake; uses emotion-laden words.
4. *Compromising*: When his own idea or status is involved in a conflict, offers compromise, yields status, admits error; disciplines himself to maintain group cohesion.	Becomes defensive, haughty; withdraws or walks out; demands subservience or submission from others.
5. *Facilitating communication*: Attempts to keep communication channels open; facilitates participation of others; suggests procedures for discussing group problems.	Ignores miscommunications; fails to listen to others; ignores the group needs that are expressed.
6. *Setting standards or goals*: Expresses standards or goals for group to achieve; helps the group become aware of direction and progress.	Goes his own way; irrelevant; ignores group standards or goals and direction.
7. *Testing agreement*: Asks for opinions to find out if the group is nearing a decision; sends up a trial balloon to see how near agreement the group is; rewards progress.	Attends to his own needs; does not note group condition or direction; complains about slow progress.
8. *Following*: Goes along with movement of the group; accepts ideas of others; listens to and serves as an interested audience for others in the group.	Participates on his own ideas but does not actively listen to others; looks for loopholes in ideas; carping.

GROUP TASK ROLES

Categories describing the types of member behavior required for accomplishing the task or work of the group.

Usually helpful	*Usually destructive*
1. *Initiating*: Proposing tasks or goals; defining a group problem; suggesting a procedure or ideas for solving a problem.	Waits for others to initiate; withholds ideas or suggestions.
2. *Seeking information*: Requesting facts; seeking relevant information about a group problem or concern; aware of need for information.	Unaware of need for facts, or of what is relevant to the problem or task at hand.
3. *Giving information*: Offers facts; provides relevant information about a group concern.	Avoids facts; prefers to state personal opinions or prejudices.
4. *Seeking opinions*: Asks for expression of feeling; requests statements of estimate, expressions of value; seeks suggestions and ideas.	Does not ask what others wish or think; considers other opinions irrelevant.
5. *Giving opinion*: States belief about a matter before the group gives suggestions and ideas.	States own opinion whether relevant or not; withholds opinions or ideas when needed by the group.
6. *Clarifying*: Interprets ideas or suggestions; clears up confusion; defines needed terms; indicates alternatives and issues confronting the group.	Unaware of or irritated by confusion or ambiguities; ignores confusion of others.
7. *Elaborating*: Gives examples, develops meanings; makes generalizations; indicates how a proposal might work out, if adopted.	Inconsiderate of those who do not understand; refuses to explain, show new meaning.
8. *Summarizing*: Pulls together related ideas; restates suggestions after the group has discussed them; offers decision or conclusion for the group to accept or reject.	Moves ahead without checking for relationship or integration of ideas; lets people make their own integrations or relationships.

ROLE PLAY TO PRACTICE OBSERVING FUNCTIONAL ROLES

Second Observation– Role Play– Preliminary Negotiations between Union and Management.

1. *Mediator from Chamber of Commerce.* You want both sides to be happy. Your goal is to arrive at a solution that satisfies both sides. It would look bad for business in town if there were a strike; on the other hand, if the word goes around that labor gets everything it wants, business will not be attracted to this city.

2. *Union Representative.* The workers must have a raise: too many are beginning to question why they pay dues. If you can't get a raise, get an equivalent. The president of the company is a nice guy if you treat him with respect (he goes for that), but you don't like to kowtow. You will if things get bad; the most important part is to come out with something.

3. *Shop Steward.* You want a raise for the workers. It makes you feel important to sit down with the president of the company and feel that you are his equal. You want to be sure he treats you as his equal. You are hurt easily by any slight; your voice must be heard. Remind them you can cause a strike, make trouble for them, etc. You want to show the workers in your plant how important you are and to get them a big "package."

4. *Company President.* You are head of a large company. You are in the midst of modernizing your equipment, which will mean more automation and laying off workers. Possibly workers can be shifted to other places in the plant but not at the same level. A small raise wouldn't be bad (profits have been substantial), but how about the layoffs next year and the possibility of a strike then? Perhaps something can be worked out, but you want them to understand that you are considering such alternatives. You are a leader in the community; you are not the equal of the working man in intelligence, education, or standard of living; you are superior.

5. *Independent Businessman.* You are a small businessman. An increase in this industry means an increase for every worker. You are just barely making ends meet; you can't afford a raise; you would be faced with going out of business. You like being on a par with the president of the large company, a prominent person in town. You certainly see his point of view better than the workers, who only care about their earnings; they are unconcerned with yours.

other for maintenance roles. A better procedure is to have two observers for task roles and two for maintenance roles so as to check reliability. Following the activity, the observers feed back their findings in the emerging roles.

Sometimes a questionnaire can be distributed to participants, immediately following the situation, in which each person is asked to state who he felt was the leader of the group, who was most influential, and with whom he would like to work again. These results are determined. There is discussion about the amount of agreement or variety of responses and why. This discussion gets at the various bases of power. Following the questionnaire the observers feed back their findings. The group examines how these results support or are different from their ratings on the questionnaires.

Discussion

What did you learn about your behavior in a group? Which roles do you usually take? Which do you wish you could take on more frequently? These questions can be listed in a short questionnaire and fed back as data to participants. There could then be sessions allowing participants to build skills in the roles with which they have difficulty.

What kind of leadership is helpful to the group? What blocks movement? These questions usually lead into a discussion of clarity—or lack of clarity—of goals. It becomes clear that we are open to the influence of only some members. Frequently, we have difficulty in putting out needed behavior for fear of its not being accepted.

3. Increasing Understanding of Leadership and Power

The following are a series of exercises that focus on various aspects of leadership and power. They are quite simple and appropriate when a group is working on some aspect of leadership, and when acquiring data on their group would be useful.

They may be used in a variety of contexts: as a warm-up for further discussion, or a theory session, as a "quickie" to help the group understand its own processes at a given moment, or as a beginning for thinking about aspects of leadership.

How Many Leaders?

Generally there are several leaders who emerge in a group: the task leader concerned with goal accomplishment, the social-emotional leader whose prime behavior is in maintaining working conditions within the group. Either of these or another may have the most influence in the group. A simple sociogram will provide data for determining who the leaders are. Each person is asked to respond to the following questions: Who has the best ideas in the group? Who is best liked? Who is most influential?

The data is gathered, tallied visibly before the group, and results determined. The group discusses findings. Is the same person the leader in all three areas or are there three different people with highest scores? What are the implications for group? What generalizations can be derived regarding leadership?

Power—In a Line

When people seem concerned about their relative influence in the group, or who is listened to and who is not listened to in terms of influencing action, this is an appropriate exercise. The facilitator simply asks the group if it would be willing to try something. If members reply, "Yes," he proceeds. He asks that all members arrange themselves in a line, with the person who sees himself as the most influential at the head of the line, and the person who sees himself of lesser influence further down the line, according to the degree of influence he feels he has in the group. Then he asks that members who believe someone is misplaced move him to where they think he should be. Then the members look at the ranking and discuss how they feel about it. If they discuss how they feel about their influence, it elicits data on how they feel about the group, its task, and their relationships with others. It can also lead to a discussion of how influence by some members could be increased, as, for example, the silent member who ranks at the tail because he rarely speaks or attempts to influence.

Higher and Lower Status

This exercise is a variation on the one preceding. In everyday conversation we may refer to someone as "the big cheese" or "a prestige member." We say of others, "Oh him," or "It doesn't matter that Bill isn't here; we can start without him." We often imply in these expressions, as well as by our nonverbal cues, that some have higher status than others (even in a so-called nondifferentiated group). High status means greater ability to influence; low status, limited ability to influence, although low status may produce negative influence.

The questions then asked are: Who has the highest status in the group? Who is next? Who has least? Members are now instructed to arrange themselves so that the person of highest status stands on a table, those of lower status stand on chairs farther out from the center. Those of yet lower status stand on the floor but also farther from the center. Those lower yet crouch or lie down, still farther from the center. Once more members may rearrange one another if they feel someone is misplaced. Members complete their hierarchy, and then discuss it. How many are in the center, what are the problems? How "far out" and how "small" do low status persons feel? What problems in the group could be reduced if this were changed? How could it be done?

A variation here is not only the height and distance relations but also a pairing and cluster relation. The exercise is the same as above, but people now also group themselves as to whose influence they are most open to and cluster around their status people.

Who Are You in a Group?

Frequently we categorize ourselves and others in dichotomies: good-bad, leader-follower, talkative-quiet. We rarely seem to see the variety of behaviors required in a group, or our own roles in them. This exercise begins to help participants see their own roles, and the roles of others. The facilitator asks members to write down their typical behavior in a group on a piece of paper. He asks that they fold the sheets and lay them aside. He then divides the group in half, naming them group 1 and group 2. He asks each member from group 2 to select a partner from the other group. The first group is assigned a task, for example, building a creation from tinker toys, or reaching a decision on the Johnny Rocco case (see Chapter III), or making a collage of the world as it may be in 1990. The members of the second group observe their partners' behavior specifically. They can be given the functional roles listing as a basis for observing. At the end of the task the observer feeds back all the various behaviors of his partner. Then members look at the earlier statement on their typical behavior and discuss it among them. Then the procedure is reversed. The second group performs a task; each member is observed by his partner. Descriptions of behavior are fed back again; they examine earlier sheets and discuss them. Finally a group discussion is held on the variety of group behaviors observed and the range of behaviors exhibited in a limited experience.

Who Would I Like To Be?

Most of us wish we could be more effective in a group. Some roles come easily, and we are skillful; others we rarely use. Each member is given a copy of the functional roles and is asked to list the roles he uses most frequently plus those he uses infrequently or rarely. The facilitator divides the group into trios. One person interviews another on which roles he rarely uses and asks why. The third person takes notes. The interviewer asks which he would like to be able to use more and what stops him, and what he might do to change. The interviewer only asks clarifying questions; responses come from the person being interviewed. The trios reverse and continue until each person has discussed the roles he takes, those he rarely takes, and those he wishes he could become more skillful in. Each person is given the notes on his interview as a basis for future planning or skill sessions.

4. Power Questionnaire

Objectives

To identify those who have power in the laboratory experience
To identify the bases for power
To understand power in subgroups as well as individuals

Rationale

This questionnaire is appropriate for distribution in a laboratory or class experience in which participants have known one another in an ongoing relationship.
The questionnaire aids participants in understanding the dimensions of power and
identifying those perceived as the most powerful persons or groups within the
larger laboratory.

Materials

A power questionnaire is needed, and it should be adapted so that groups on the
second page represent groups within the laboratory (see page 67). Also needed
are newsprint, magic markers, tape for analyzing data, and, if desired, material
for theory session or handout on power.

Design

Participants are asked whether they would like information on who are the most
powerful members of the laboratory, and which are the most powerful subgroups.
The facilitator may explain power as a concept and explain the bases for power
so that members are more aware of different kinds of power. (If the participants
vote against receiving such information, the design should be omitted.)
The questionnaire is distributed. Participants are asked to fill it in and given time
to do so (about 15 minutes).
Someone collects the data and calls it off to another who is standing at the newsprint and records. When a person's name is called, he is listed on the newsprint, a
tally placed by his name, and the reasons on the right-hand side. Each question
is tallied separately, and the tallies totaled.
Members respond to the data before them.

Discussion

Who is the most powerful person in the laboratory? On what is his power based?
Who is the least powerful person (this is a noninfluence relationship, not a negative influence)? Why?

POWER

As a group, or an organization, exists over time and the members meet to carry out their business, a working structure forms. The form may be different from how it was intended to work; it may be different from how it worked in its earliest formative stages. At a critical period, as it meets a crisis, who are the "haves" and who are the "have nots" becomes increasingly evident. If we can examine the influence structure at these critical times, we can better:

1. Understand the bases of power at this laboratory (with possible interpolations to the general society)
2. Examine the implications of power as it affects the individual, interpersonal relations, and the goals of the community
3. Understand the dynamics of a change in power, if it comes, and on what basis, by the end of the laboratory

Power is generally defined as the ability to meet the needs of another. More specifically the person with power (P) has power over another (O) in a specific area (X). A person can have power over another only because he can meet the needs of another in a specific area. Or, it is only because O has needs which can be met by P that gives P his power.

Questions arise as to who has power to make decisions on the planning of the laboratory and the content of the work projects. Are all heard equally? Who has greater influence? On what basis? Is power one-way or two-way?

French and Raven have defined five kinds of power.

1. Reward power (ability to meet the needs of another by reward- a raise, praise, etc.)
2. Coercive power (ability to coerce- to fire, ridicule, to downgrade, etc.)
3. Expert power (ability to meet the needs of another due to superior knowledge in that area- engineers who know how to build a road, staff who know how to run a laboratory, etc.)
4. Legitimate power (people holding positions or representing others- a representative from each change agent group to work on community problems or social issues)
5. Referent power (Who are the people you refer to or defer to? Whose opinion do you ask? Whose advice do you seek?)

QUESTIONNAIRE

The following questionnaire is designed to help better understand power in this experience.

1. Who are the five people who influence you the most? Next to each name, briefly state why. (List in order of influence: 1 for most influential, etc.)

    Name   *Reason*

2. Who are the five people who influence you the least? Next to each name briefly state why. (List first the person you are least influenced by.)

3. Who do you think you influence most? Briefly describe why. (List first the person you think you influence most.)

4. How much influence do you think you have in this laboratory? (Check on scale.) Why?

    ```
    L_____|_____|_____|_____L
    None                                                      A great deal
    ```

5. Assume that a decision needs to be made on future laboratory activities. By which group would you be most influenced in making your decision? (List 1 for group which would influence you most; 2 for second most influential, etc.) Briefly give a reason.

    Black participants   Training staff
    Spanish participants   Females
    White participants   Males

6. In your opinion, who has the most power in this laboratory? Briefly state why. (List 1 for most influential, 2 for second, etc.)

    Black participants   Training staff
    Spanish participants   Females
    White participants   Males

How accurate were your perceptions of the person you influenced?
What blocks your influence? How does this compare with others' interpretations of your influence?
Which subgroups are most powerful? Least powerful?
How would you generalize your learnings about power?

5. 64 Squares—Different Leadership Styles

Objectives

To learn how leader behavior influences the members
To experience differences in social climate due to differences in leadership
To increase understanding of leader behaviors at points on the decision-making continuum, and choices a leader can make
To understand some of the phenomena revealed by the classic Lewin, Lippitt, White studies on leadership and social climate
To increase understanding that leadership styles influence productivity

Rationale

Sixty-four squares is basically a small replication of the Lewin, Lippitt, White (1939) leadership study. Controlling for personality (the same person enacts all three leadership styles) and difficulty of the task, the exercise directly examines the influence of leadership style on climate and member relations as well as group productivity. The experience, especially because it controls for personality variables in the leader, frequently produces dramatic learnings and new realizations that leader style very much influences the entire group.

Setting up the Situation

The facilitator should spend some time briefing the person who will enact the leader roles. His portrayal is crucial to the entire exercise. Frequently a colleague is enticed to take on this role; however, it can be anyone familiar with the original research. The groups meet in the following order: first the "autocratic" group, then the "democratic" one, and finally the "laissez-faire" one. The leader is reminded of the essentials of each role:

   The *autocratic* leader is directive. He controls the interaction; he begins the meeting, calls on people, insists the "chair" be recognized, and does not permit conversation or discussion among participants. He sets up the agenda, gives only one step at a time, and does not permit deviation from the agenda. He states what he considers the method to solving the problem from the beginning.

   The *democratic* leader shares decision making. He outlines the problem, permits the group to decide its method. He participates in the discussion, but does not direct it. He may give suggestions. He is supportive of others in the group.

The *laissez-faire* leader maintains a minimum of participation. He comes in, sits down, does not speak unless someone asks him a question, and then he answers only that question.

On the blackboard or on newsprint, the facilitator sets up a large square divided into 64 smaller squares.

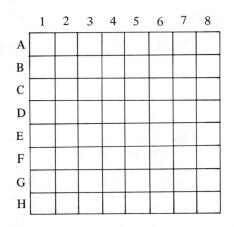

The facilitator asks for 15 volunteers to make three groups of five each. He selects the volunteers and asks all of them to go into the hall. A table is set up with six chairs where all of the participants can see and hear.

A timekeeper is selected. He is instructed to record the amount of time it takes for each group to arrive at a decision on a procedure. A recorder is selected. When the group implements his procedure, he records the number of questions needed to arrive at the correct answer. He is instructed in his role. The facilitator asks that a square be selected to be "it." It may be decided that "E-5" is "it." This becomes the object for the discussion groups, who seek to find the block that is "it."

Each group is to agree on a procedure to find the block that is "it." Once they agree on the procedure, they must use it until they obtain the correct answer. The others in the room will tell them when they have the correct answer.

Design

The facilitator asks five persons and the leader to come into the room and be seated at the table. The leader will be the same person in each situation, and in the first group he will enact the role of the autocratic leader. The facilitator states that the group must establish a procedure to determine which block of the 64 squares has been selected to be "it." After the procedure has been agreed upon, the discussion takes place. The group uses the procedure to ask questions in order to determine which block is "it." The length of time taken in the discussion is recorded; the number of questions required to get the correct answer is noted.

The players join the audience. The next five are called in and seated at the table with the leader, who now enacts the democratic role. The facilitator gives the same instructions as in the autocratic role play. The group has a discussion and finds the block, the time, and the number of questions noted, as in the previous situation. The five players join the audience. The next five are called in, and the leader joins them. The leader enacts the laissez-faire role. The facilitator describes the task as previously; the group proceeds and the observers report back as in the other two situations.

Discussion

Members of each group are asked how they felt working with their leader, and why. This exercise is dramatic in developing an understanding that one physical person can be responded to in such varying terms depending on his leadership style. Members of the autocratic group feel controlled and describe him as dominating and very difficult to work with. The laissez-faire group frequently see him as incompetent, as weak, and as "wishy-washy." They often report frustration in not even having a clear understanding of the problem and feel they wasted a great deal of time. The autocratic group reports a hostile atmosphere, and participants report conflict with the leader or giving up and withdrawing. Usually the members of the democratic group agree that they would like to work together again.

The facilitator asks participants to compare the results of the observer's findings. Which group was most efficient, i.e., which needed the least time for discussion and the least number of questions to determine the answer? Which group was least efficient? Are there implications in these differences? Usually the autocratic group, by a small margin, is the most efficient. However, since the members did not like working with one another or the leader, what are the implications for a group working in the short run? In the long run? For more information the reader might refer to the findings of the study.

Which group was most productive, i.e., needed the smallest number of questions to arrive at an answer? Sometimes a group may require a long time before it reaches a decision and arrives at a procedure, but then implements it quickly and efficiently. There is then a general discussion on how leadership style influences the working climate and the relations among members.

6. Decision Making along a Continuum—Problems

Objectives

To experience some of the roles people play in decision making
To experience ambiguity with a leader and note how it affects both the process and the product
To understand the choice-of-leadership continuum, and its implications for members
To increase understanding that a leader-member relationship is a dynamic one, each previous relationship affecting the present one
To increase observational skills of a dyad in change

Rationale

This exercise has very dramatic learnings. It becomes obvious that the leader-member relationship is a fundamental one in understanding group process and organizational functioning. The leader and member roles are defined, much as they frequently are, and the leaders have more direct access to instructions from the top than the members. The information members receive is based on how the leader decides to transmit it—whether limited, ambiguous, or honest. Although the leader becomes more member-oriented in his decisions, the member may not perceive himself as having a more significant role. He may be reacting to previous behaviors of the leader, and he might have developed a lack of trust and an apathetic response. Participants become aware of the dynamic relationships in a group, i.e., that members' trust of the leader influences the degree of work in decision making, and that clarity in decision making is an important factor in leader-member relations. It also permits members to understand the effectiveness of multilateral versus unilateral decision making.

Materials

There should be three lists of innocuous items to be rank-ordered. (The lists are not of importance in themselves; they are simply a basis for discussion and decision making.) Some examples are: What are the most important qualities of a good teacher? Ten qualities are listed, with a dash as a place for ranking before each item. Qualities might be: education, initiative, creativeness, persistence, fairness, a sense of humor, diligence, love of teaching, interest in travel, experience. Other similar questions are: Rank these 10 presidents as to their importance in history. Then the names of 10 presidents are listed. Another example: Rank these people in order of the importance of their contribution to mankind: Charlemagne, Julius Caesar, Socrates, Martin Luther, Galileo, Darwin, Shakespeare, Queen Victoria, Karl Marx, Adam Smith.

Three different lists are required, and there should be two copies of each list, preferably on differently colored paper. One color (let us say green) should always be given to the leader; the other color (white) should always be given to the member. There should be enough lists for two-thirds of the participants. There should also be sheets printed for observers. The sheet is headed Observer's Sheet and should list questions to direct the observer's attention to the data to be gathered. For a sample of the Observer's Sheet see page 73. These sheets are needed for one-third of the group.

Action

The group is divided into trios. One person is the leader, one the member, and one the observer. Each trio will be asked to perform three ranking tasks and to turn in their decision on each, according to specific instructions. Following the third exercise, observers report back their findings, and leaders and members respond with their feelings on the situations. This is followed by a general discussion.

The group is again divided into trios and told that they will be asked to perform three tasks, each of which involves reaching a decision. In the tasks, the participants are to maintain the *same roles* throughout, i.e., the person who is the leader will continue in his role as leader in all three tasks; the person who is the member will occupy that role for all three tasks; the observer will maintain that role in all the tasks.

Instructions are given at the beginning of each task. However, prior to giving instructions, the members are asked to leave the room. Only the leaders receive instructions, as frequently happens in many groups and organizations. Instructions are then transmitted from the leader to his member or subordinate. It is important that the members leave prior to instructions so as to avoid the psychological effect of feeling left out, and because they should not know the changed rules for each task.

TASK I

Instructions are given to leaders; members are not in the room. The leaders are instructed that they and their paired member will each be given a list of items to rank-order. (The leader is given the green sheet, the member the white sheet.) Each person will rank the items individually. Then the leader and member will discuss the lists between them. No attention is to be given to the member's list. At the completion of this task, the leader will only turn in the list he made. No mention is given to the member's list. Members are not told about the special instructions. The leader may discuss his list with the member in any way he likes, but only his list represents the final selection. Observers will not participate. They will be concerned with gathering observational data. Members are called back in. The leaders and members take their sheets and rank the items individually. The facilitator announces that the group has 20 minutes to work before each group is asked to submit a list. The groups work on the task; at the end of 20 minutes the leaders turn in their sheets.

...re asked to leave
...g instructions. They feel
...t always is"; the members are
...e extent the leader wants to relay in-
...sed" since the leader paid no attention to their
...y his own ranking. Leaders often feel that they
...th members, frequently leaving members with expectations
...s a disillusioning experience to find suggestions were not con-
...This discussion is not brought before the group. It is developed here so that
...e facilitator may understand some of the dynamics developing in the relationship.

TASK II

Members are asked to leave the room; instructions are given to the leaders.
The leaders are instructed that they and their paired member will each be given
another list of items to rank-order. However, this time they are to use a fair
and equitable decision-making process. They are told to adequately consider
the member's list so that a collaborative ranking is developed. They are told
not to mention their special instructions to the members. The members are
called back in. The leaders and members take their sheets (a new listing but
maintaining the same colors for leaders and members) and again rank the items
individually. The facilitator announces that the groups have 20 minutes to
work before each group is asked to submit a list. The groups work on the task;
at the end of 20 minutes joint sheets are submitted.

Discussion

The member once more feels left out, but he feels it more acutely following the
unilateral decision making just experienced. His feelings about the leader may
range from strong anger at being manipulated to "you can fool some of the people
some of the time, but you won't fool me again." He will be more guarded, and less
willing to be involved in the task. He may feel the leader is pressuring him; he may
be verbally antagonistic to the leader. He may see the leader turn in a joint list, or
he may still feel the leader is turning in his list. It is important to note that the
member's subjective reality greatly influences the climate of the group as well as his
relationship to the leader.

TASK III

The members are again asked to leave the room; as previously, instructions
are given only to the leaders. The leaders are again instructed that they will be
given a list of items to rank, as will the members. Once more the new lists are
distributed on the same colored and white paper. The instructions to the
leaders now are, "The list you turn in really does not matter, because we will

Discussion

The facilitator should be aware of how members feel when they
the room and how they feel about only the leaders receivi
left out, apprehensive. They feel that "this is how i
given the information secondhand and to th
formation to them. They also feel "
suggestions and submitted on
should discuss issues
of influence. I
sidered

Task III:

Task II:

Task I:
mer

throw it away. Let the members turn in whatever they want; their list will be the one representing the group. Once more do not tell the members of these instructions."

Members are asked to return. The members and leaders take their lists and rank them. The facilitator announces that each group will work on its task and will be asked to submit a list for the group. Usually this takes about 10 minutes. The members submit their lists.

Discussion

The members become even more annoyed at being left out of the instructions. Attitudes toward the leader are mixed. In some groups they are beginning to reconsider their relationship, partially and somewhat grudgingly. In other groups, the relationships are strained and viewed as a "personality clash." However, now the leader acts either apathetically or seems to be pressuring the member in order to influence his list. The relationship is ambiguous. The level of involvement is low, effort on the task is greatly reduced, and the climate is characterized by minimal communication and maximal suspicion. Although the member has more influence in making the Task III decision, he neither knows nor is involved at this point. The actions of the leader leave him confused; he is increasingly less sure of his own role.

General Discussion

Following the three tasks, the group observers report back on the behaviors they have seen. Leaders and members respond with their feelings on each of the situations. There can be a discussion with the entire group related to their reactions in each of the situations, the level of involvement, and their feelings about the group as a whole. Discussion can be in terms of how participants felt after each task, and perhaps they can generalize some of the learnings.

The following questions might be the basis for general discussion: How do people feel about multilateral versus unilateral decision making? Both the leader and the member experienced a task in which each made decisions irrespective of the other; they also experienced a time when they shared the decision making. How does it affect both the process (the degree of involvement) and the product (how good do the participants think their list was)?

How did the members feel when they were asked to leave? Why? (Allow time here, since feelings are generally quite strong.) How did members feel about the leader? Why? What are the implications for working with ongoing groups? What are the implications of this exercise for decision making in a group? What behaviors are helpful? Which hinder?

7. Leadership Questionnaire

Objectives

To enable participants to share their expectations of a leader
To stimulate discussion on the role of a leader
To increase understanding of the role of a group member
To increase learnings on current theory in leadership research
To examine behavior for its implications in a group

Rationale

There is probably no area in which there are such mixed expectations as in the area of leadership; yet somehow we assume that all the other members have the same expectations we have. This exercise is an appropriate one to use as an opening experience in a group. It serves to further examine leadership and leader-member roles. It allows participants to deal with not only expectations but also consequences of various behaviors. For many it may represent the first time that they have seriously considered alternative modes of leadership behavior in lieu of the consequences of a given answer to a problem situation.

Materials

The materials needed include the Leadership Questionnaire (see page 77), newsprint, and magic markers to record the group decisions.

Design

Members are divided into groups of 6–8 and preferably seated at a table.
Copies of the Leadership Questionnaire are distributed to each participant.
Each person is asked to think about his understanding of leadership and to answer the questions true or false independently. (As always a bit of humor helps. "No cheating" evokes smiles. A statement like "Decide whether you are going to put an *x* in the box or a check—this is the time of decision" serves to relieve tension and put participants in a more communicable frame of mind later.) Allow about 10 minutes.
 The facilitator asks members to discuss their answers. In their discussion they are to:

1. Consider the implications for a group if the answer is true and if it is false. What would be the short-run consequences? What would be the long-run consequences?
2. Determine which answer (true or false) best represents your group *after discussion.* (Allow about 20 minutes.)

LEADERSHIP QUESTIONNAIRE

1. In the case of a stalemate, a leader can facilitate group problem solving by making the decision for the group.

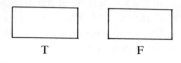

2. Sessions planned by the leader tend to be more efficient than those planned by the members.

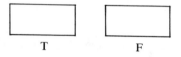

3. A group should not expect a good leader to always take the responsibility for clarification of the problems facing the group.

4. Leadership training will never produce leaders if leadership personality traits are lacking.

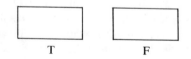

5. It is up to the leader to put a member in his place when the success of the group is endangered by his behavior.

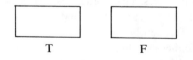

Sheets of newsprint should be placed on the wall, with each sheet labeled for a different question, i.e., question 1, question 2, etc. The facilitator then asks that the groups report their decisions on each question with an accompanying short reason for each reply. These are recorded on the newsprint. In the discussion following responses to each question, the facilitator should take a devil's advocate position if there is agreement in the group replies; if there is disagreement, the participants should be encouraged to further amplify their reasons for a position. In the discussion following question 4, the facilitator should state research findings with regard to traits of leadership. (It is important for members to understand that there are no invariant traits of leaders.)

Discussion

Discussion frequently gets quite heated, especially when members are asked to agree on a group answer to the questions. Many of the problems of leaders inadvertently come to the fore. Here the reader should refer to the Questionnaire. On question 1, a standard reply for a true answer is, "That's how it's always done." This answer leads into the problem of, "Do we do it as it has always been done?" or "Do we examine the implications of such an action? What does being bound by tradition mean; is it freeing or rigidifying? Which? When?" On question 2, a true answer is justified as an orderly meeting with a planned agenda. Consider efficiency as high productivity over a brief time. What are the problems when the leader plans the meeting in terms of his needs? What are the problems of a leader separate from the membership? Question 3 is in sufficiently ambiguous wording to provoke a variety of issues. One is the question of, "Is there a good leader as against a bad leader, and what are the differences?" Perhaps the leader should not always take the responsibility for clarification of problems, but for all practical purposes he should. This leads into the subject of what the leader's role is and what the member's is. Question 4 never fails to evoke polarization. There are those who say, "You are born with the magic 'it,' and without 'it,' true leadership can never be attained. Leaders are born." Others say, "Traits can be trained." The questions are: "What are the traits of leaders? We don't know." "What are the implications of this theory; how do we feel about that?" Question 5 is another that says, "The leaders get the glory and also the dirty work." A true response is justified in that the leader wants his term to be a success, and so he must squelch blockers. The question is, "What is the leader's role, and what is the member's role?" Assume this situation in a classroom. Which is more effective? Which is most frequently used? Why?

Following the recording of replies and discussion on each of the questions, the facilitator can lead a discussion with the entire group, or he can provide some questions for the groups to discuss at their tables. Which approach is used will depend on the size of the group, the time available, and the goals to be focused on in subsequent leadership exercises.

1. What expectations do we have of leaders? How realistic are these expectations?

This is an especially appropriate question when the participants consist of "leaders." They readily discuss that they feel inadequate, that the burden of leadership is too much, that they fear failure.

2. How can leadership-membership become more a joint venture?
    After some general discussion, participants are asked to list specific ways for leadership to be shared.

3. What blocks each of us from becoming more influential in this group? This question gets into what is theoretically permitted as opposed to what behaviors are actually considered safe. It will also get into a number of membership issues, such as importance of membership, reasons for membership, attractiveness of the group, etc.

4. Questions from the early part of the discussion, which examined some possible replies to questions and their implications and which are especially an issue for the participants, can be used as discussion questions and further developed.

Variations

1. The facilitator appoints an observer to observe members as they attempt to arrive at a common answer for each question. The observers may be instructed before the exercise or may be given written instructions. In either case they are to notice:
    What is the leadership pattern? (Is discussion controlled by one or a few? Are responsibilities shared?)
    What is the basis for leadership? (Is leadership based on position in this organization, an outside position, high verbal behavior?)
    The observer takes notes and reports back his findings to the group after they are recorded on newsprint. The group then discusses the feedback from the observer.

2. An observer is appointed as above, and his duties are the same until the time to report back. Now, instead of reporting his findings, he asks the group the following questions: Who do you believe influenced us most? Why was he the most influential person?
    The participants are asked to write replies to these questions. The observer reports his observations. The replies from the group are read. There can then be a check as to the amount of agreement within the group. Usually there is no agreement, since each of us may be open to different kinds of influence. The facilitator may from here present a brief theory session on different kinds of power: referent, expert, legitimate, reward, coercive. It helps to clarify differences in perception and different bases of power as well as illustrate the fact that we determine who influences us and to what extent.

6 exercises in group problem solving and decision making

Overview of Exercises

1. *The Horse Trade* Given limited time (5 to 10 minutes) to solve what appears to be a rather simple mathematical problem, there is a tendency for participating groups to revert to nonfacilitative behaviors when they are unable to arrive at immediate agreement. Issues of power, control, and the mechanics of the decision-making process are easily viewed within this context.

2. *The Multiple Dot Test* Asked to reach consensus on a task (the group is allowed one answer in deciding how many dots exist on a piece of paper or how many beans are in a jar), a variety of helpful and nonhelpful behaviors are generated. The exercise is a good one for opening the group to initial issues relating to the problem-solving process.

3. *The Water Jar Experiment* How well a group uses its resources and is able to build cooperative decisions can be observed as the participants struggle with this problem of mathematical measurement. The exercise is ideal for helping to introduce a group to the concept of "process" and how process observation can be useful to a decision-making group.

4. *Objects off the Table* Again, this exercise provides an ideal opportunity for a group to focus on a range of problem-solving issues after a brief but intense decision-making task. The task itself involves issues of cooperation and sharing.

5. *The Hollow Square: A Task in Creative Problem Solving* This activity is very useful in helping participants understand the tensions inevitably produced when individuals from different levels of an organizational hierarchy (subordinates and superordinates) are drawn together into a decision-making process. Leadership, patterns of communication, and conflicting roles are easily identified as crucial areas that may reduce group effectiveness.

6. *The Peg Board Game: Decision Making under Pressure of Time* Decision making under extreme pressure can exaggerate the kinds of problems that tend to reduce group effectiveness. This exercise involves the participants in a simple, mechanical task that requires team strategies for the best results. With two or more teams competing, other variables are introduced that can be analyzed systematically by the groups after the task is completed and observational data are presented.

7. *The Nonzero Sum Game: A Test of Trust in the Problem-solving Process* Most organizations are established in a manner that maximizes competition both internally (among members) and externally (in relation to other organizations). This exercise focuses on the destructive aspects of this reality and

how untested assumptions are all too often the basis of decisions. The exercise is ideal for helping groups understand issues involving trust and in-group, out-group status within an organization.

8. *The Chairman Role: Dealing with Conflict in a Group* In this activity participants are helped to develop insights concerning the role of an effective group chairman. Through the analysis of feedback data on effective and ineffective role behaviors of the chairman, those involved are able to design and practice new approaches.

9. *Compass and Mapping Orientation* How much do individuals with influence and control over a situation willingly seek involvement of others in the decision-making process? That is a key question raised in this activity which places individuals in a stress-producing situation (lost in the woods) with the goal of finding their way to safety together.

10. *The Five Beam Puzzle* This activity can be used to serve many of the same purposes as those described previously. It requires no more than 10 or 15 minutes to complete, yet it generates a broad range of participant behavior which can be used to involve the group in a discussion about problem solving and decision making. It combines the need for physical and intellectual cooperation.

11. *The Acid Floor Test* This simulation design can be used with a single group or with a large number, competitively or noncompetitively. The situation is such that the group will tend to develop rapid and premature solutions without drawing on the needed resources of the entire group. It often leads to failure and frustration by those participating when ideas "pushed through" with little thought prove ineffective, and makeshift alternatives are developed to compensate.

12. *The Devil's Dilemma: Combining Reality and Creativity in the Problem-solving Process* This design enables groups with real problems to participate in a stimulating series of activities that insure high levels of involvement and critical thinking within the problem-solving process. It also encourages people to consider the positions and supporting values that lie behind diverse viewpoints in the group. Finally, the process is one that takes the usual drudgery out of problem solving while still being very task-oriented.

13. *Role Reversal: A Means of Unblocking a Polarized Group* By encouraging participants with opposing viewpoints to take the roles of their opponents, group members are able to realize how little communication is actually taking place between the opposing factions. Until what is being heard is separated from what is being said, little can be done to resolve the existing problems. This exercise helps move individuals away from their own positions so that new understandings may be gained and new positions forged.

14. *The Ideal Program: Movement from Old to New Ideas* The aim of this activity is to spring participants loose from old positions and to help them consider alternatives. The hope is to stimulate new and creative viewpoints without forcing individuals to explain all of the "hows" behind the implementation of each idea. It is a positive period of exploration without commit-

ments of any kind—a testing of the wind and viewing of creative possibilities without defensiveness.

15. *The Open Chair: A Means of Insuring Greater Group Participation* Too often large group discussions become unwieldy and unproductive. A usual complaint is that it is the ideas of only a few that get heard, and there is no opportunity to gain fresh ideas once individuals have clarified their own positions. This activity helps to insure that new ideas and opinions are not locked out of a group discussion while also insuring the advantages of a small-group discussion.

16. *The Newspaper Interview: A Means of Discovering the "Real" Issues in a New Group* This activity enables the facilitator to raise feelings, attitudes, and concerns in such a way that group members can share them in a relatively nonthreatening manner. By doing this, the facilitator may find his meeting plan is inappropriate in terms of "where the group is." In addition, the design helps increase the facilitator's credibility with the group as a result of dealing openly with such issues.

17. *The Process Diagnosis: A Means of Altering Group Behavioral Patterns* This exercise is directed at familiarizing a group with methods for observing its own process in a relatively nonthreatening manner. By helping the group generate and analyze information about its own pattern of work and involvement, it is possible to develop more effective alternatives. The questions used are merely examples of the kinds found to have a high impact value and which create potential discrepancies between what is happening in the group and what individuals would like to happen.

18. *Maslow's Hierarchy of Needs: A Means of Understanding the Problem of Creating Open Communication and Feedback within a Group* This activity manifests the fact that it is usually extremely threatening and thus difficult for individuals to look at their own needs and concerns and to deal with them openly. By providing the group with a vehicle to overcome this difficulty, it is possible to move individuals from an intellectual understanding of group process to one which incorporates both intellectual and emotional dimensions.

NOTE: It is clear that a great many of the exercises discussed previously have direct or indirect implications in relation to problem solving and decision making. It is impossible to think of roles, norms, or communication patterns in isolation from the problem solving. An alert facilitator will be able to adapt many of these to a discussion of problem solving that focuses on a key issue with which the group must come to grips.

Introduction

Ideally, by the time a group explores the area of problem solving and decision making, an understanding of other aspects of group process has been achieved. Problem solving represents an integration of many concepts into an action framework.

The issue becomes one of assuring the best mix of all the component parts. Thus norms, roles, leadership, goals, and patterns of communication all play a vital part in how effectively a problem is resolved and in what manner the eventual decision is determined. For this reason, many of the activities recorded in this section could be easily adapted as a means of studying one of the other aspects of group process.

The exercises are grouped into three rather natural areas of investigation. First there will be a presentation of activities that provide a group with the opportunity to look carefully at its own problem-solving process and the inhibiting and facilitating factors generated in reaching decisions. Simulations, games, and puzzles are all used as a means of distinguishing how groups behave under the pressures of a particular task. Second, methods for facilitating group decision making will be outlined in a manner that allows for replication in a variety of group settings. And, third, specific exercises are developed that focus on the evaluation of the decision-making process. Again, inherent in almost all of the exercises is a means for group evaluation of what occurred during the activity. Many of these methods can easily be applied to actual group problem-solving sessions in which the group is interested in evaluating its own behaviors and procedures.

Activities for Viewing the Problem-solving Process

Following are a number of brief exercises designed to produce information concerning group problem solving in a few minutes. These activities will involve the participants in intense problem-solving situations. When used with discretion, these activities provide insights into the issues that tend to prohibit effective problem solving. Characteristic patterns of behavior develop rapidly when the participants are placed under severe time constraints and when they are challenged by a tantalizing test of their own problem-solving abilities. Again, it should be noted that an enormous amount of information will be available in a short time, and it will be up to the facilitator which part of the data should be given attention. It is quite possible to overwhelm a group with too much information and too many implications, and the potential learning offered from the exercise is lost.

1. The Horse Trade

Setting

The participants are broken into groups of from four to six. They are told that they will be given a problem that they must solve independently of the group, and they are instructed to write their answer on a piece of paper. Once each member of the group has done this, instructions are given that members must now solve the problem as a group and derive one answer that can be agreed upon by all participants. They may not use voting, but must listen to the reasons of the various individuals and then arrive at some joint decision. They will have 5 minutes for the task (at the most 10). The facilitator may wish to have a process observer in each group observing certain specific aspects of the participation such as (a) How are ideas accepted and how are others rejected and on what basis? (b) Is the climate such that individuals feel free to communicate their ideas, or do they capitulate to individuals with power, charisma, knowledge, or certainty? (c) Who talks the most and who talks to whom? (d) Does a true consensus develop among the members? Much of this information may prove of secondary interest to the actual data collected, and what kind of information is collected depends on the specific objectives of the session.

Action

The following story is read slowly and clearly to the group. The subject matter could easily be altered to fit a wide range of groups. A certain embellishing of the story and a sprinkling of humor will usually enhance participant involvement.

> A poor farmer comes into what for him is a lot of money- $60. He decides to buy a horse to alleviate his plowing burden which previously had been done behind a lame mule. With the plowing done, he sells the horse for $70 and uses the money for seed. Still later, after his harvest, he buys another horse, but this time for $80. However, shortly thereafter his wife becomes ill, and he is forced to sell the horse to pay doctor bills. The farmer receives $90 for the horse. How much does the farmer gain as a result of all of these transactions?

Discussion

The problem is such that there should be a natural dispersion in responses between $0, $10, and $20, although other responses are frequent. Without giving any indication of the correct answer ($20), the facilitator records the participants' responses on the board or newsprint. He then asks for the single answer from each group and also records this in view of the participants. The learning for the large group lies in a discussion on how it is that some groups have the wrong answer and yet within the group at least one person had the correct answer. Persuasion, coercion, power, and other factors that "pushed" the decision in a certain direction are considered. It may be helpful to have each group spend a few minutes looking carefully at just how it reached its decision, whether all of the resources in the group were used, and how people felt about the discussion that developed before the decision. At this point, a process observer could inject his observations. (It is also helpful to have the individual participants note their feelings of involvement in the decision, or their satisfaction with the decision, by using rating scales immediately after the decision is made; this information can then be tabulated and discussed.) The facilitator will want to have some of the groups share their observations and the implications they hold for problem solving.

2. The Multiple Dot Test

Setting and Action

This exercise may be used independently or in conjunction with the previous one. For example, instead of a single problem for the small groups, they may be given two. The second one (the first being the Horse Trade) would be to have the participants look for 20 or 30 seconds at a piece of paper covered with a large number of dots and representing no particular pattern. Each individual is to note the number of dots he thinks are on the paper. Now each group is given approximately 10 minutes to solve both problems. The groups often methodically attack one and leave little or no time for the second and resort to problem-solving processes so characteristic of many groups: either the quick vote, a process of averaging, or the opinion of the most vocal member. It is important to emphasize the necessity of solving both tasks (if this is the design of the facilitator). Again, there is a correct response available, and the groups are able to quickly become aware of many extraneous factors in their decision process.

Discussion

Such an exercise is more useful in raising important questions and sowing the seeds of further discussion than for attaching too much importance to individual behaviors. It can be used nicely to stimulate further investigation, but the facilitator should not overplay his hand in an attempt to impress the group with all of the potential learnings.

3. The Water Jar Experiment

This exercise is primarily used to get a group of individuals involved in a common problem. It can be used effectively as a first step in developing work skills in the decision-making and problem-solving process. How the facilitator focuses on the behaviors that occur is up to him. The main thing, however, is to realize that random observations of such a task are seldom helpful unless the observers are extremely skillful and experienced in group observation. Often it is better simply to raise some critical questions for the groups to look at together and, if possible, discuss the implications of data gathered by a process observer or by the group as a whole. The members of small groups (four to six members) are asked to solve the following problem as rapidly as possible. Often it adds interest and excitement to make the task competitive among the various groups. The facilitator might suggest that this is the first meeting of a group that will continue to meet over time in a problem-solving capacity.

Action

The following problem is presented: If you have a seven-quart jar A and a four-quart jar B, how can you obtain exactly 10 quarts of water.

There should be a definite time limit. When members have arrived at an answer, they report to the facilitator who then records the time (if the answer is correct) on the board. (This adds pressure to the remaining groups.) Before the groups are allowed to discuss the process aspects of the activity, individual members should respond to a number of questions concerning the work of the group on paper and return it to the facilitator without their names but with their group number. The questions should be designed to raise questions and not answer them. The following suggestions may prove helpful:

1. On a one-to-seven-point scale (with one being not at all and seven being completely), indicate how involved you were in the solution of this problem.
2. On a one-to-seven-point scale, indicate how much you would like to work with this group again in solving other problems.
3. Briefly describe your two strongest feelings during the time the group was solving the problem.

Discussion

From only these three questions, considerable information can be developed. For example, it will be noted (assuming there are a number of groups) that in some groups all or nearly all of the members felt highly involved and in other groups only one or two felt involved, with a conspicuous gap in the feelings of the remaining individuals. This may have nothing to do with their success in completing the task. The implications from this piece of information can be discussed in the small groups or in the total group.

From the second question it is inevitable that there are some groups in which the majority of the participants would not want to work again. Why should this be the case in such a short period of time? Why should some individuals in one group desire to work again in that group and others in the same group not desire it? The participants will begin to realize that in ongoing groups success in decision making also involves how the participants feel about the process. If individuals are not happy, one might ask how this could influence their behavior the next time.

Finally, a look at the range of strong feelings coming from the various groups will dramatically suggest just how strongly people feel (both positively and negatively) about what occurs in the problem-solving process.

Solutions

Fill jar A, fill B from A (leaving 3 quarts in A), empty B, fill B from A. Thus 3 quarts are obtained by the rule A − B, and the additional 7 quarts from A; (A − B) + A = 10.

4. Objects Off the Table[1]

Setting

Participants sit around a table. On the table are a number of objects that would have some appeal. For example, for a group of eight there might be three different kinds of candy, a piece of gum, a quarter, a dime, and an inexpensive ballpoint pen. The rule is that after a period of 2 minutes, the members are free to take an object from the table. The one they take becomes theirs. The only other information given is that they are involved in a problem-solving activity. No other directions are allowed.

Action

With one less article than there are people, an immediate point of tension is created. Also, with articles of differing value, some process of selection or allocation is necessary. The group may decide on a tension-reducing process of randomly distributing the items and leaving the decision of who gets nothing to chance. This, of course, is a failure on the part of the group to take responsibility and to recognize that the desires of individuals may help, not hinder, the resolution of the problem. Thus, by choosing a minimum strategy few members will stand to be pleased by the process, but also, fewer will be disappointed. A choice of greater risk lies in the attempt to discuss alternatives and to work against the competitive nature of the members. In addition, there is the real possibility that individuals will begin to label certain items as their own. For example, one person may see the ballpoint as the item representing greatest worth and status and decide that either he is going to obtain it or no one will. Or another person seeing an object of relatively low value will put his mental stamp on it because while this object may be valued less in the group, it will still enable the person to come away with something. One way to establish these preselection priorities is to have the individual members rank their first two choices on a piece of paper during the 2 minutes prior to the discussion or action phase of the task.

Discussion

It is very helpful to have process observers for each group, but they should be given very specific observational tasks. Post-task reaction sheets covering a variety of feelings about what occurred during the decision-making process can also be used to give participants some direction in their analysis of the events. A few questions aimed at the task groups can open a stimulating discussion around the complexities

[1] This exercise was adapted from experiments conducted by M. M. Flood in 1951 while at the Rand Corporation and reported in *Decision Making,* W. Edwards and A. Tversky (Eds.), Baltimore, Md.: Penguin Books, 1967, p. 53.

of the problem-solving process. Each group might be asked to generalize the feelings and experiences of this exercise for other task-oriented problems and then share this information with the larger group. Process data may also be of interest in the total group because of the different strategies developed in different groups.

5. The Hollow Square: A Task in Creative Problem Solving

Objectives

To stress the importance of developing interest and involvement among subordinates in tasks that depend upon them for success
To indicate how easily control and domination can develop in what is supposed to be a shared task
To explore the implications of clear communication and channels of leadership in a problem-solving task
To build an awareness of general factors that seem to inhibit the problem-solving process

Rationale

In almost every type of organization there are tasks that require the giving of orders and directions by administrators (in this case planners) to those who must implement the orders (in this case operators). Clear communication and skillful planning are absolutely essential if the job concept held by the administrator is to be carried out by the subordinate. This simulation activity provides an opportunity to look closely at problems that arise in virtually any teacher-pupil relationship.

Setting

The activity requires a minimum of three groups. First, there is a Planning Team of from five to eight participants (under optimal conditions). Second, there is an Operation Team of from five to eight participants. Finally, there is an Observer Team with from two to six participants. Ideally, two or three sets (each with a Planning, Operating, and Observation team) of teams take part at the same time, thus increasing the competitive atmosphere and inducing a wider variety of problem-solving behaviors among the participants. It is best to have the Planning and Operating teams in separate rooms during the initial phase of the design.

General Overview of the Exercise

Members of the Planning Team are each given a set of detailed instructions. They are also given the 17 pieces of a puzzle which when properly assembled form a hollow square design. The pattern of the design outline is also given to the Planning Team. They are told that they are responsible for instructing the Operating Team on how to implement the Planning Team's plan for assembling the 17 pieces into the shape of the hollow square. At no time is the Planning Team allowed to put the puzzle together. The Planning Team is given from 25 to 40 minutes (depending on the facilitator) in which to plan its strategy for helping the Operating Team. They may call the members of the Operating Team to join them in the planning session at any time, but, when they do, they are no longer able to have the design outline before them. During the last 5 minutes (at least) the Operating Team must be present with the Planning Team to receive its instructions. (See the detailed briefing sheets for further details, pages 91–93).

Observers should be present during all of the planning and implementation phases, and at least one observer should be with the Operating Team as it waits to be called by the planners for instructions.

Although the Observation Team has rather detailed instructions for observation, the members should have a fairly detailed briefing prior to beginning the activity. Even with this detailed information available for later discussion, it is helpful for the facilitator to look for a number of possible occurrences. For example, it is quite common for the Planning Team members to become so involved in the process of solving the problem that they forget that their goal is to instruct the Operating Team in the best possible manner. All too often the Operating Team sits waiting to be called by the planners for most of the planning time. When it is finally called, the planners might well have forgotten to assign a single person to give a coherent picture of the task. Further, with only a few minutes left to explain the task, there is confusion. The planners may be too busy explaining, and there is little time left for questions from the Operating Team which, by then, may be highly anxious from having waited so long.

Thus, the exercise focuses directly on the issue of shared decision making, developing subordinate rapport in the learning-instruction process, as well as on issues involving roles, norms, and leadership. When the task is completed, members of the Operating Team should be given brief questionnaires to determine their feeling of involvement, interest, and satisfaction in the proceedings. Also, it is helpful to have them briefly note how they would change the process now that they have been through the learning and implementation phases.

Discussion

Groups of six, including observers, planners, and operators, are useful for discussing what happened and the implications for other groups. A larger group session might be used to explore the evaluation data collected from the various Operating Teams. Another possibility is to have the Observer Team form an inner circle and discuss what they saw happen, while the other participants sit around the outside and listen. After the data have been shared, the circle can be enlarged to include members of all three groups to further explore the implications of the data.

Time

The entire exercise runs a minimum of 2 hours and can easily run for 3 hours if the observers have done their job and the participants are given an opportunity to look beyond their own experience in order to generalize their learnings for other groups.

BRIEFING FOR OPERATING TEAM

1. You will have responsibility for carrying out a task for people according to instructions given by your Planning Team. Your Planning Team may call you in for instructions at any time. If they do not summon you before ____, you are to report to them anyway. Your task is scheduled to begin promptly at ____, after which no further instructions from your Planning Team can be given. You are to finish the assigned task as rapidly as possible.
2. During the period when you are waiting for a call from your Planning Team, it is suggested that you discuss and make notes on the following:
    a. The feelings and concerns you experience while waiting for instructions for the unknown task.
    b. Your suggestions on how a person might prepare to receive instructions.
3. The notes recorded on the above will be helpful during the work group discussions following the completion of your task.

BRIEFING FOR PLANNING TEAM

Each of you will be given a packet containing _____ cardboard pieces which, when properly assembled, will make a hollow square design.

Your Task   During a period of _____ minutes you are to do the following:
1. Plan how the 17 pieces distributed among you should be assembled to make the design.
2. Instruct your Operating Team on how to implement your plan (you may begin instructing your Operating Team at any time during the planning period– but no later than 5 minutes before they are to begin the assembling process).

General Rules
1. You must keep all pieces you have in front of you at all times.
2. You may *not* touch or trade pieces with other members of your team during the planning or instructing phase.
2. You may *not* show the blue sheet (with the detailed design) to the Operating Team at any time.
4. You may *not* assemble the entire square at any time (this is to be left to your Operating Team).
5. You are *not* to mark on any of the pieces.
6. Members of your Operating Team must also observe the above rules until the signal is given to begin assembling.
7. When time is called for your Operating Team to begin assembling the pieces, you may give no further instructions, but you are to observe the operation.

BRIEFING FOR OBSERVING TEAM

You will be observing a situation in which a Planning Team decides how to solve a problem and gives instructions to an Operating Team for implementation. The problem consists of assembling 17 pieces of cardboard into the form of a hollow square. The Planning Team is supplied with the general layout of the pieces. This team is not to assemble the parts itself but is to instruct the Operating Team on how to assemble them in a minimum amount of time. You will be silent observers throughout the process.

Suggestions for Observation

1. Each member of the Observing Team should watch the general pattern of communication but give special attention to one member of the Planning Team (during the planning phase) and one member of the Operating Team (during the assembling period).
2. During the planning period watch for such behavior as the following:
   a. The evenness or unevenness of participation among Planning Team members.
   b. Behavior that blocks or facilitates understanding.
   c. How the Planning Team divides its time between planning and instructing (how early does it invite the Operating Team to come in?).
   d. How well it plans its procedure for giving instructions to the Operating Team.
3. During the instruction period (when the Planning Team is instructing the Operating Team), watch for such factors as:
   a. Who in the Planning Team gives the instructions (and how was this decided)?
   b. How is the Operating Team oriented to the task?
   c. What assumptions made by the Planning Team are not communicated to the Operating Team?
   d. How full and clear were the instructions?
   e. How did the Operating Team members react to the instructions?
   f. Did the Operating Team feel free to ask questions of the planners?
4. During the assembly period (when the Operating Team is working alone), watch for such things as these:
   a. Evidence that instructions were clearly understood or misunderstood.
   b. Nonverbal reactions of Planning Team members as they watch their plans being implemented or distorted.

HOLLOW SQUARE PATTERN

When properly assembled, all the *pieces* make up the following pattern:

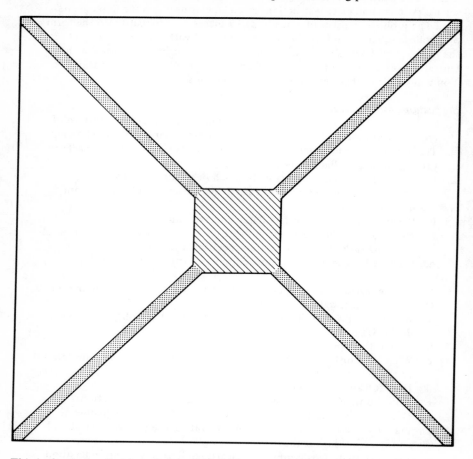

This is the design that is to be given to the Planning Team and which they must relinquish at the time they call their Operating Team in for instructions. [NOTE: it could easily be given up after a short time. However, wanting to solve the problem, and perceiving themselves as the experts, the tendency is for the planners to hold on to the design (control) as long as possible- forgetting the needs of the operators.]

DIAGRAM OF ASSEMBLED HOLLOW SQUARE

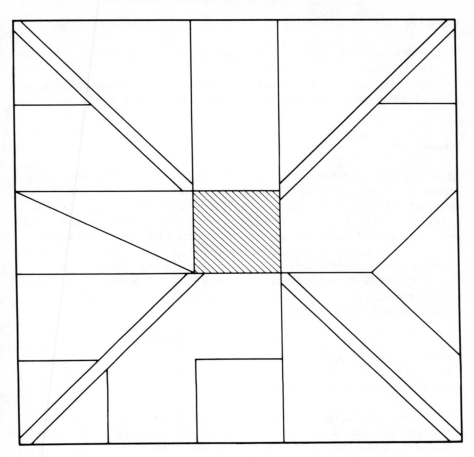

(For the use of the group facilitator)

6. The Peg Board Game: Decision Making under Pressure of Time

Objectives

To provide a view of the decision-making process and the execution of a task under extreme time pressure

To begin understanding how individuals respond to such pressure and how this often inhibits problem solving and influences the eventual decision

Setting

As in many of the exercises in this section, this one provides observers with the opportunity to practice sorting through an enormous amount of observational data and to try and determine the major factors that influence a particular decision. A table is placed in the middle of the room (it should be no more than perhaps 6 or 7 feet across) without chairs around it. Five or six participants are asked to stand around the table and await instructions. Others in the room are simply asked to watch the process carefully and take any notes they feel may be helpful in the later discussion. (The facilitator might, of course, decide on some particular dimensions to observe, and he could brief the viewers on particular observational roles.) A second group will then repeat the task.

Action

The following directions are given by the facilitator:

I will describe a task for you to perform. You should know that when you first learn the nature of the task, it may appear to be very simple, but it is not. Actually it is very difficult because of the element of time. You will want to spend considerable time planning how to execute the task, since once you are told to begin, your success will depend on the strategy you have worked out. There may be a tendency to develop one method and refine it. This will prevent you from thinking of creative alternatives, one of which may be a better method. Your effectiveness as a group will depend on your speed in completing the task, based on a record of other groups that have attempted the task, and based on another team from your own group which will have an opportunity to better your time. Winning or losing may be a matter of only a few seconds. Again, think of as many alternatives as you can and then select the one approach that appears best and refine it. Here are the directions. Please listen carefully since I can give them only once, and there will be no questions. You will have time to plan. When you have completed your planning, I will present you with a peg board- a board with holes in it. I will give you enough pegs to fill all the holes. Your task is to insert the pegs in the holes in the shortest possible time. During your planning period you cannot use any visual aids (the blackboard, pencil and paper), even the use of your hands. You must plan by verbal discussion only. The planning period begins now.

Since the participants have not seen the board, they may doubt the existence of one. They will tend to flounder for a while unless a very strong leader begins to take over. After observing the group plan for a period of time (this may vary with the particular group but usually occurs after 5 or 10 minutes), the facilitator says:

You seem to be having some difficulty in your planning. Perhaps it would help if you saw the actual peg board. [At this point the actual peg board, a flat board about 10" to 12" square and with 100 1/8" holes evenly spaced in rows is placed on the table in front of the group.] It also might help if you had the pegs for the board. I will distribute them among you [the facilitator should distribute them unevenly among the members.] Now you have the board and all the pegs. As you continue your planning you may do anything you wish except touch the board or exchange or redistribute the pegs among yourselves. Let me know when you have reached a point where you feel ready to perform the task. I will then give you the signal to start and time your performance for comparison to the other groups.

If, after 5 minutes or so, the group still has not completed its planning, the facilitator can say:

I don't feel that much progress is being made. Apparently you could go on this way all night. I'm going to impose a 5-minute [or 10-minute] time limit. At the end of that time, you must be ready to perform the task.

The facilitator times the group and records how long it takes for the members to place all the pegs in the holes. At this point he assembles another group around the table. Basically the same procedure is followed, although, since these members are already familiar with the exercise, they will probably be given the board and pegs within a shorter period of time. There should be a distinct difference in the two groups, the second being more facilitative in their behaviors. Often, however, with the pressure to outdo the first group and feeling the need to "look better," the second group listens less, pushes through a rapid decision, and generally fails to apply themselves to the task.

Discussion

The large group is divided into subgroups with at least one member of the two participating groups in each. The facilitator asks each group to share the observational data of its members and also to interview the individual who had participated in the peg board game. They are to look for critical similarities and differences in the two task groups that attempted to solve the problem. Finally, the discussion groups should try to make generalizations from their data for other decision-making groups. After about 30 minutes, the findings of these discussion groups can be shared in a meeting of the total group. Then the facilitator brings closure on the shared learnings, perhaps in relation to some theoretical concepts of problem solving and decision making that seem particularly applicable.

7. A Nonzero Sum Game:[2] A Test of Trust in the Problem-solving Process

Rationale

This fascinating and frustrating game draws out and focuses on the tensions created by the competitive nature of many organizations. It faces squarely the need for trust within the framework of organizational decision making and shows how easy it is to mistrust the motives of the other person. It reveals that the tendency is to think the worst (negative) in a situation where there is an equal chance for a positive or negative response on the part of the other party. Often the game establishes a clear cycle of suspicion and distrust (based primarily on untested assumptions) leading to more suspicion and distrust. Even when this suspicion leads to a non-winning strategy, there is often a tendency to pursue it just so long as the other person *also* fails to benefit. A major assumption of the game is that a majority of people will try to establish a winning strategy at the expense of the other person or team. If this strategy to maximize one's own position is taken by both teams in this game, then neither team is rewarded as much as if they had taken a more cooperative position. Cooperation is the key, not competition.

Setting

Two teams consisting of 6 to 10 players each are selected (the teams may be familiar or strange in their orientation toward each other; it depends more on the aims of the facilitator). While the activity is basically a two-team game, it is possible to have two or more games (total of four or more teams) going simultaneously in the same room. The room itself should be large enough to have the two teams grouped together about 30 feet from each other. They should be visible to each other, but they should not be able to hear each other (except for the natural laughter or groans that may develop during the course of the activity). There should be a messenger-observer available for each team. His role is to take messages from one group to the other and to note the specific verbal dialogue that takes place among members of his group, thus building a historical picture of values and feel-

[2] This game is adapted from two sources: Luce, R. D. and Raiffa, H., *Games and decisions: Introduction and critical survey,* New York: John Wiley and Sons, 1957, pp. 94–102; Deutsch, M. Trust, trustworthiness and the F scale, *Journal of Abnormal and Social Psychology,* 1960, *61,* pp. 138–140.

ings as they are generated during the course of the game. The teams should have a large score sheet (newsprint size) on which the score of their team and the other team is recorded after each round. As noted on the sample score sheet below, there are eight rounds in the game.

	1	2	3	4	5	6	7	8
Black Team								
Red Team								

Directions for the Participating Groups

All of the participating teams should be assembled in one place for the directions, which should be given only once and as clearly as possible. The teams then go to their respective locations in the room and are given 5 minutes to discuss the directions and the objective of the game. At that point they are expected to take their first-round choice. The facilitator says:

> Your groups are taking part in what is known as a Nonzero Sum Game. Please listen carefully to the directions since they will be given only once. You have been divided into two groups for the purpose of this activity, a Black Group and a Red Group. Each group has a score sheet with places for scoring eight rounds of the activity. The number of points you earn is determined by the choice made by both groups, that is, the Red Group and the Black Group. The Black Group will decide between *X* or *Y*, and the Red Group will decide between *A* or *B* [at this point participants are shown the Grid on page 100].

Again, the number of points for each group will be determined by both groups for each round. For example, the Red Group will look at the Grid and decide whether to give the Black Group an *A* or *B*. This choice is written on a piece of paper and given to the messenger, who gives it to the Black Group. At the same time, the Black Group members decide whether they will give the Red Group an *X* or *Y*. Once they decide, they too give their response to their messenger, who transfers it to the Red Group. Round 1 ends when each group has received the response from the other and has entered the appropriate points on the score sheet for both teams. Based on this information and other points of discussion in the two groups, round 2 would then begin, and each group writes a response for its messenger.

Further Information for the Facilitator

1. On p. 100 is the Grid used as a basis for making decisions within each group and from which scores are calculated. Each group should have a Grid that is easily visible to all members of that group.

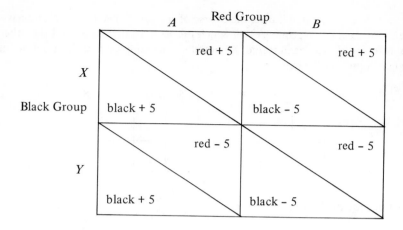

2. If, during the first four rounds, there is any indication of tension, mistrust, suspicion, and even hostility between the two groups because of their strategies, the following procedure might prove useful. Each group is told after the fourth or fifth round that there will be 5 minutes to decide prior to the next round whether they wish to: (a) have a brief meeting with the other group; (b) have a spokesman from each group meet and represent their groups in a discussion of the events along with any proposals; and (c) exchange notes. At least 5 or 10 minutes should be allowed for the implementation of a particular course of action by the two groups. It may happen that there can be no agreement on these possibilities. In that case, the next round should proceed.

3. A bit more clarification on the Grid may be helpful. The numbers in each cell represent the consequences for the groups having selected that particular cell. For example, the upper left cell (*X - A*) represents the logical combination of strategies in which each group agrees (implicitly) upon a less than optimal strategy, since each group has the risk of losing –5 points. Thus, it is a risk or a cooperative strategy that is taken in hopes that the other team will wish to maximize the position of both sides. But, if the upper right cell is the choice, it places the Black Group in the position of the "sucker" since Black "trusted" that Red would not take a strategy that could hurt Black. Thus, Red chose the strategy in which it might lose –5 points, but it also might stand to win +5 while Black was losing –5 if Black chose the *X* strategy. For the Red Group, the *B* strategy is "safe" since it can do no worse than break even with Black. Using the same line of reasoning, had Black chosen *Y* as a strategy and had Red chosen *A*, then the Red Group would be the "sucker." It should be noted that all the feelings about winning or losing, playing safe or cooperatively assumes a competitive viewpoint on the part of the players. But the description of the activity in no way suggests what it means to win or lose or what is the "best" score. It is possible that a low score could be considered best since it might mean that the group trusted and did not try to retaliate with a defensive strategy as

the game progressed. There are many ways in which the game could be interpreted—it is the groups who make it competitive along the lines of win and lose.

4. If it is apparent that the two groups (or even just one) have developed a competitive viewpoint, it is often interesting to look at the game in terms of point totals. If, for example, it can be assumed that plus points are good and negative points are not good, it might appear obvious that teams would desire to maximize their potential point total. If both teams had decided on a cooperative strategy rather than a win-lose one, through the eight rounds, they would have each received 40 points. This virtually never happens. If, on the other hand, both groups had been completely distrusting, both teams would receive –40 points. This too seldom happens. But the degree of trust and the willingness of the two teams (or one) to cooperate can be seen clearly in the score sheets. This provides a useful point of departure for a large group discussion.

Discussion

Reports back from the messenger-observers can be amusing and most enlightening. They should be able to sketch for the total group (Red and Black) the development of their group's strategy and how trust or mistrust was generated (i.e., out of which untested assumptions). If they have noted exact statements made in the groups, it is possible that in round 2 someone will say, "Watch out, they'll get us next time," "We'd better get them before they get us." Later in the game there may be such statements as "I wonder if they'll kick us again while we're down," or "This ought to finish them off."

Game type activities frequently are criticized by players who complain that they are simply not real. This may be so, but individuals tend to act characteristically when there are pressures similar to those in the real world. The statements often generated in this unreal activity attest to the fact that reality for them is the game, and their attitudes and strategies parallel those we witness every day.

Alternative Design

A slight twist in the procedures can lead to slightly different conclusions. Instead of having the two groups make each of their choices independently and based only on the previous behavior of the other, the Black Group can make its first decision and then give it to the Red. It is then up to the Red Group to make its decision based on the decision of the Black Group. They (Red) then make the next decision as well and Black receives it. Then based on Red's behavior in round 1 and its behavior in round 2, Black makes its decision in its round 2 choice, which will decide the actual distribution. The game continues in this vein and creates an even greater dependency (and potential hostility) between the two teams. In this process the blows are more direct than in the first procedure.

8. The Chairman Role: Dealing with Conflict in a Group

Objectives

To practice diagnosing and working with a framework of conflicting viewpoints in a problem-solving group
To generate alternative chairman behaviors in situations where vested interests of a personal nature seem as important as the task that has been defined by the group

Setting

This activity involves a six-person role-playing situation in which various members of the group are coached in positions for and against a particular point of view. The chairman is to help the group reach agreement on certain specific recommendations involving the disputed issue. The design is based on a situation in which there is an even number of teams taking part in the role-playing scene. For purposes of this discussion, it is assumed that there are four groups of six players each; each group is enacting the same role play and has its own chairman.

Each group will take part in the initial role play simultaneously for approximately 30 or 40 minutes. The chairman, who is working under a time pressure, attempts to facilitate the group in any way he can. After the allotted period of time, the individual groups analyze the sources of conflict and the ways in which the chairman did and did not help the situation. Then they outline other procedures that might facilitate the chairman's role in a similar situation. At this point, one member of the group is sent to another group, and the previous chairman takes a member role. Thus, group 1 will have a chairman from group 2, and group 2 will have a chairman from group 1 (the same switch will occur in groups 3 and 4). At this time, group 1 reenacts the role play with the new chairman, and group 2 observes. After about 15 minutes, group 2 reenacts the scene with its new chairman. Both chairmen try to include the suggestions raised in the discussion after the first role play. Groups 3 and 4 are doing the same thing. After the second reenactment, the two groups discuss their observations and draw a number of generalizations concerning the chairman role in situations of conflict; these are then shared with the total group (all four groups). From 2 to 2½ hours should be allowed for the activity.

Action

The facilitator makes a general statement on the objectives of the activity and then proceeds to give a general description of the role-playing situations.

You are the members of a junior high school faculty in a deprived area of the city. On returning to school on a Monday morning, it is discovered that vandals (apparently students from the school) have caused damage in a

number of classrooms. Worse than this, however, the windows of the rooms
of three teachers have been defaced with obscenities. Since these rooms overlook the playground and the parking lot, nearly all of the students and the
faculty saw what was written. The school is in an uproar, and there is no end
of talk about "why those particular teachers" and who could have done it.
There is also some fear that such behavior could lead to much worse problems
in the future.

The principal is outraged and takes immediate steps by appointing a six-man
faculty committee to investigate the incident. If possible, they are to discover who the culprits are and recommend punishments for the acts. The
principal has given the committee 2 days to submit a report with their recommendations.

SPECIFIC ROLES OF THE SIX COMMITTEE MEMBERS
(Name cards are needed)

Mr. Simmons (Chairman). You have been appointed chairman by the principal. You tend to have a liberal outlook and believe that there
must be good reason behind the "selective madness" of the
student vandals. Beyond your personal views, you are anxious
to be an effective chairman, and you realize how important it
is for both students and faculty that a fair decision is reached
by the committee. As chairman, you begin the first meeting by
saying: "Our principal asked me to chair this committee. . . ."

Mr. Vincent You have been appointed to the committee as a representative
of modern elements in the school. You are well respected for
being able to act as a harmonizer and integrate diverse points
of view. You are not considered a person out for personal
power or gain, and you have the trust of most of the faculty. You
do have strong opinions and are not afraid to express them, but,
on this issue, you have very mixed feelings and do not enter
with a firm position in mind.

Mr. Paul You are often perceived as antiadministration and anti-
establishment. You tend to see students as pushed down by the
system, and you think that, in many ways, the administration
is guilty of the pent-up frustration many students feel. In the
past your outspoken views have gotten you into trouble. In
fact, you know that a promotion was rejected because of your
strong position on one occasion. Actually you are attempting
to mend fences and want to be perceived as less extreme so
that possible promotion may come your way, and put you in a
position whereby you can be more effective in changing those
conditions that seem to inhibit the learning process. At this
moment you feel very anxious about your role in this meeting.

Mr. Peters You take a strong stand in defense of whoever did this thing.
It is your belief that only very angry and frustrated persons
could have done it and that they are more in need of help than
punishment. The environment is to blame, and you personally
believe that the three maligned teachers contribute more than

their share to that environment. Also, you know one of the culprits well, like him, and respect his family. This could be a scandal to them. For these and other reasons you wish to see what happened as a symptom of a larger problem that needs to be attacked with vigor.

Mr. Johnson (Assistant Principal) As the administration's representative on this committee, you feel that something decisive must be done as a deterrent to further problems of this nature. You are more concerned with how you are perceived in an administrator's role than anything else and realize that your performance will be carefully observed by the principal, who has a strong vested interest in immediate aciton. You do not like friction and find personal confrontation difficult to take. This is a problem because the principal is a very confronting person and admires directness and toughness in people.

Mrs. Smith You personally feel that the children involved must be punished and taught a lesson. Not only does your security as a teacher depend on this, but severe punishment is the only possible vindication for the three teachers (two of whom are close friends). You have been in the school for a long time and feel resentment at the changes you have witnessed during the last 5 years. Not only have academic standards deteriorated, but discipline has almost vanished in the classroom and in the halls. In your mind, the only way to handle these students is through immediate and severe action.

Warm-up

The facilitator has the individuals playing the same roles in groups 1 and 2 and in groups 3 and 4 spend a few minutes practicing and shaping their roles so that they enter the discussion with some conviction and involvement.

Second Role-Play Session

After the discussion of the first role play, the chairman, Mr. Simmons, takes the role of Mr. Vincent in each group. Now, the original Mr. Vincent goes from group 1 to group 2, and from group 2 to group 1, and takes over the chairman role that has been vacated. He attempts to implement new approaches to the problem and the various conflicts that appear to exist.

Discussion

After the conclusions of groups 1 and 2 and 3 and 4 have been shared with the total group, the facilitator may find the following questions and observations helpful in bringing further issues to the surface or in summarizing the various issues.

Should the chairman be neutral or take a substantive position?
Have the decision-making procedures been defined for the group? Who has made this decision?
What approaches has the chairman used to reduce personal goals and develop a shared group goal?
Was there an opportunity for individuals to release personal feelings without polarizing the group further?
What efforts have been developed to insure more data for the committee in its deliberations?
Given the urgency and short time, how could the most efficient use of the group's resources be insured?

Special Problem-solving Activities that Require Physical Activity or Need to be Held Outdoors

Following are a number of activities that require either special facilities or plenty of room, usually in an outdoor setting. By adding a physical dimension to the task and enforcing strict time limits, the participants find it very difficult to avoid full involvement and, as might be expected, they tend to generate the characteristic behaviors seen in most stress situations. Because members must be interdependent in these exercises, they provide an effective means of looking at the decision-making process and also for building teamwork among a group of individuals.

9. Compass and Mapping Orientation

Objectives

To force a group in a foreign environment to discover appropriate resource people to help it solve its particular problem
To observe how various individuals respond to the stress of unfamiliar surroundings and an unfamiliar task, especially those with high control needs

Setting

Participants (usually groups of from five to eight) are blindfolded and driven to an unfamiliar location (woods and fields preferably) and told that lunch or dinner is awaiting them at a spot approximately one mile away. They are given a geological survey map of the area and a compass. A person who knows the area stays with the group, but he is given instructions not to help except in emergency situations. It is up to the group to learn and work together.

Action

The participants' blindfolds are removed, the location is noted, and a few materials are provided. No other instructions are given. This is a particularly interesting exercise for people raised in the city and for whom such an experience can be threatening.

Discussion

The group should be helped to focus on such questions as the following:

Were the real resource people in the group used?
Was an attempt made to help the other members of the group become involved in the problem-solving process, or were they left to follow and assume little responsibility?
How was leadership manifested in the work of the group?
What tensions were created fron interpersonal factors, and what tensions were created out of environmental factors?

10. The Five Beam Puzzle

Objectives

To develop problem-solving skills in a group, particularly to build an action plan before committing the group to that action
To observe the development of leadership in a competitive problem-solving situation
To facilitate team building among a group of strangers

Setting

Six log stumps of approximately equal height (1–2 ft.) and at least a foot in diameter are located in the pattern diagrammed below. Five wood beams are laid on the ground beside the first stump. There are three beams (4"/4") which are 8 feet long, and one that is 10 feet long, and one that is 12 feet long. The object is for the group to decide how it can make a path along the stumps with the beams and then get all of the group members to the other end without touching the ground. The exercise is timed and usually competitive.

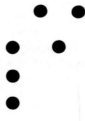

Action

The following directions are given by the facilitator:

You will observe the six stumps that are more or less in a row. Your task is to place the five 4"/4" beams so as to reach across the stumps and form a pathway that will enable your group members to walk to the other end. Several rules should be noted. First, no person may touch the ground at any point between the various stumps. Second, no beam may touch the ground. Each one must be placed on the stumps. Once the route and method have been worked out by the team and a team member has successfully made his way across, he may return (on the ground) and give a hand (one hand) to those who find it difficult to walk the beams without help. If a person goes off the beam at any point, he must return to the end of the line and repeat the maneuver. Your effort is being timed, and other groups will be competing with you. Your time begins now.

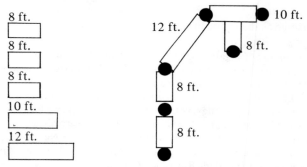

(The solution is to place the first four beams as shown above and then lay the last 8-foot beam so that one end touches the middle of the 10-foot section and the other end touches the last stump.)

Discussion

Time should be available for the group to discuss how the problem was solved. How could they have worked more efficiently, and would this have influenced any of the decisions made during the period of problem solving? Did haste make waste in this case, and was time given to develop a reasonable strategy with all of those who might have something to contribute, given the opportunity? It is possible that specific issues relating to leadership or membership, etc. might have risen to the surface. If so, they should be explored with the group.

11. The Acid Floor Test

Objectives

To analyze decision making and problem solving under extreme time pressure
To develop supportive roles within a group
To observe individual behavior under stress—both facilitative and inhibiting

Setting

This task is more effective when it is done competitively. If there are enough materials available, as many as three or four teams of from six to ten players can participate at the same time. If materials are limited, competitiveness can be achieved by placing a time restriction on the exercise (each team works in isolation). For each group that participates it is necessary to have available eight empty no. 10 cans. It is also helpful to have observers assigned to each group to watch carefully the nature of the problem solving that takes place, how resources in the group are maximized, and how leadership develops within the context of the activity.

Action

The facilitator gives the following directions to the team(s):

> You are members of a gang that has taken a short cut across another gang's territory. You have been spotted by one of their lookouts and are aware that they are mobilizing a group of some thirty boys to come after your small group. You have decided to cut through an alley that leads to your own territory. Halfway down the alley you see that the other gang has spread acid across the alley. It stretches at least thirty feet or more ahead of you. You realize that it is too late to go back the way you came. Near the point where the acid begins the group sees a number of large cans. They see the cans as offering a way over the acid. But how? Can they figure how to get all of their gang over the acid before the other gang arrives?

There are some specific rules. No part of a person's body may touch the acid floor. If it does, he must return to the starting point and bring his cans with him. No person may sacrifice himself and run through the acid setting up cans. When the last person crosses, he must bring the cans to the far side with him so that the pursuing gang cannot follow over the acid.

This event is timed.

Discussion

By teams, the observers describe how they saw the decision-making process develop. The group may be asked to comment on these observations and discuss what might have been done better. Why or why not were other alternatives developed? Was there dependence in the group on one or two people? Why? Was there consideration for all the members of the team? Was their performance (going across on the cans) ridiculed, or was there a supportive, all-for-one attitude?

Exercises Aimed at Removing Roadblocks to Group Productivity

These exercises, if used at the appropriate time, will help a working group overcome particular problems that appear to be reducing its ability to meet its goals.

12. The Devil's Dilemma[3] : Combining Reality and Creativity in the Problem-solving Process

Objectives

To stimulate a creative problem-solving session
To help the participants face directly the kinds of realities that often keep good ideas from getting off the ground
To insure maximum participant involvement

Rationale

Problem-solving sessions all too often become so serious and tense that participants stop enjoying what should be, in many cases, an exciting and innovative process. On the other hand, many planners and problem solvers get carried away with the creative process and forget the kinds of here-and-now realities that prohibit the execution of many ideas. The think-tank approach to problem solving is usually too removed from the source of the problem, and critical factors are often overlooked. The intent of this exercise is to make sure that reality is tested again and again throughout the entire problem-solving process and that participants have an enjoyable time while working.

Setting

This particular exercise can be conducted with a minimum of 7 or 8 individuals to as many as 60 or 70 (depending on some adaptations to the design presented below). An ideal number ranges between about 16 (two working groups) to about 24 (three working groups). The use of three groups provides a most stimulating design possibility and allows for the effective use of intergroup competition and a great assortment of ideas. Below is an outline of a three-hour work session that is part of an all-day workshop. The reader will be able to alter the time schedule and numbers involved to suit his particular needs. In this case, it is assumed that the group of 24 participants has come together to work through a variety of problems. The morning

---

[3]The authors are indebted to Clark Abt, who developed the original design from which this exercise has been adapted.

session is being devoted to a single problem of importance to the entire group (how this problem is arrived at and defined may be another "problem").

Action

The members of the large group are divided randomly[4] into four working groups (names should be known or name tags provided). Actually, three of the groups will work at the task, and one group will be composed of "devils" (devil's advocates) who will help the various work groups test the reality of their ideas. The work session is scheduled to begin at 9:00 A.M. of which the first 30 minutes is an informal coffee session. The facilitator feels that by 9:30 all the participants will have arrived and be ready to get down to serious work.

9:00–9:30 Arrival of participants, coffee, informal talking.
9:15–9:30 Directions to those individuals (6) selected to be devils and assignment of groups to other members. The devils will play a key role in the success of this session and must clearly understand their function and its implications in the decision-making process. Two of these individuals are assigned to each group (it is also possible to have all six moving freely among groups, but this may prove confusing). As the discussion develops around the problem, issues may evolve that reduce the effectiveness of the group. The devil can bring these to the attention of the members. This cannot be done verbally; it must only be done by writing a note to the group and letting members respond to it among themselves. This keeps the devil in the role of an objective observer interested in the group process and asking questions he believes need to be raised. Obviously too many notes to the group could be disruptive and eventually ignored. Discretion calls for a limited use of this role. Examples of the kinds of interventions are many. For example, the observer may make observations about time, the fact that only a few people seem involved, that the group is stuck on a few ideas and has not explored other possibilities, or that they are straying from the topic into irrelevant areas. Or the devil may question a certain conclusion- in other words, actually take the role of someone outside the group who may be affected by a particular idea or decision. This gives the group a chance to test reality from an outside perspective. The following are a number of interventions that a devil might make during the planning session.

[4]If the issue represents a polarization of views in the group, it may be interesting and useful to build one group with members of similar opinions, another group with members of opposing views, and a third group composed of individuals with mixed opinions. Very often the solutions of the three groups are quite similar once all the "realities" have been considered, and once the groups begin to plan and stop being defensive over their particular positions.

1. You are talking about solutions before you have defined the problem clearly.
2. You have spent a half hour talking about an issue that can be worked out later.
3. I represent an administrator. I question your estimation of cost; it may be twice your figure if you consider training costs.
4. Three people in the group have somehow not had much of a chance to get an idea in edgewise.
5. Time is getting away from the group. Perhaps it would help if you spent some time brainstorming particular solutions, without evaluating any of the ideas until later.
6. I represent a subordinate in the company. You are assuming that I will not resent spending additional time on this task. I am already overburdened, and I do not believe you have taken my feelings into consideration. Depending on how you present the idea to me may determine my level of acceptance or hostility to the proposition.

Thus, the devil must occasionally help paint a more complete picture for the group. His statements must be objective, directed at helping the group clarify an issue, or aimed at facilitating the communication and decision-making process among the participants. Again, moderation in the number of inputs will give them greater value and effectiveness.

9:30–9:45   The problem is clearly defined (again, it is assumed that the problem is of interest), and a schedule is presented. The schedule should be placed on newsprint in view of each of the working groups.

Schedule: 9:45–11:15   problem-solving session
            11:15–11:30   break
            11:30–12:30   presentations
            12:30– 1:45   lunch break
             1:45– 2:15   summary of morning session
             2:15– 5:00   afternoon program

At this point, the role of the devils (other names for these participants may be preferred) must be clearly explained, and it should be stated that their purpose is to help the group with their own work process and also to test reality in terms of their specific proposals.

9:45–11:15   It is during this 90-minute session that the problem is discussed, analyzed, and proposals for its solution developed. By 11:15 each small group must have a plan it can present to the total group outlining intended action and the steps to be taken for their implementation.

11:15–11:30   This is scheduled as a break, but it will also enable groups that have not completed their task additional time. The facilitator should also meet with the devils for a few minutes to outline their role during the next hour. (See below.)

11:30–12:30   Group presentations will be made. The presentations themselves (with the help of newsprint) should take no more than about 5 minutes. During the remaining 15 minutes allocated to the first planning group, the total group of devils will be able to criticize the group's ideas. These individuals are instructed to respond to the ideas presented as if they were outsiders who may be influenced by the proposal. Thus, one of them can say, "But, as a person who is going to be influenced by this decision, I resent not having been involved in the planning and decision-making process."

Or another devil may say, "As an administrator, I see no place in your implementation phase for accountability. Who is going to see that your plan is actually implemented, and who will be responsible for its overall success or failure? The plan seems sound otherwise."

These comments should be heard without comment from other observers, although the group members making the presentation can reply to the role-played questions. Other members of the group who are observing may also frame questions in a similar manner. The point is to raise the kinds of questions that could result in the failure of the particular proposal. The facilitator will probably have to help keep the discussion within the proposed framework, otherwise the time will not be sufficient. If all the questions have been discussed, the presenting group may wish to accept suggestions that would strengthen their proposal. The three groups proceed through this process Thus, each has time for a presentation, an opportunity to clarify certain points, and a chance to hear the kinds of criticism that might well be generated once the proposal was implemented.

12:30–1:45   It is suggested that a representative of each of the three problem-solving groups and two of the devils have lunch together. With the previous discussion in mind, it is their task to integrate the various ideas into a plan that can be presented back to the total group after lunch. There should be considerable overlap among the proposals so as to ensure the possibility for integrating the three proposals. This is not easy, and the facilitator may wish to help the group in the organization of their task.

1:45–2:15   Often it is difficult after lunch and a morning of hard work to motivate a group into further work. This is not usually the case when the lunch-planning group presents its integrated proposal for action to the other members. During its presentation, the large group may raise some serious questions that require more work. If they cannot be resolved on the spot, it may be possible to allow this work group to reconvene and consider

alternatives that will satisfy the criticism, while the other
group members continue with the afternoon program. Hopefully, this will not be necessary. Early closure brings a real
sense of accomplishment and new vigor to the afternoon program.

13. Role Reversal: A Means of Unblocking a Polarized Group

Objectives

To help group members gain a broader problem-solving perspective
To help a polarized group with a particular issue on which certain members are
especially intransigent

Setting

If, regardless of the facilitating methods used, a group is making little progress in
reaching a joint decision because of strong differences of opinion, it is often helpful
to pull individuals away from their defensive positions. This can be done by introducing a role-play situation where the participants are either (*a*) asked to argue from
the point of view of the opposition or (*b*) design a solution that is as far as they
could go in satisfying the opposing position.

Action

A group that has moved from open discussion and the presentation of ideas to one
of defensive debate is doomed to failure, frustration, or both. The facilitator may
wish to give the group members a short break (often merely changing the physical
scene can help) so that they have a chance to move away from the positions they
have taken. Sometimes members may wish to come to a compromise position, but
the strength of their argument has boxed them into an all-or-nothing position. It is for
the facilitator (or a skilled member of the group) to help remove this barrier. Thus,
on returning from the brief break, members of the group are asked to think for a
few minutes of the opposing positions being expressed. The discussion begins, and it
is evident that many of the arguments on both sides have not been heard as the
members argue those issues that are most difficult for them to accept.

At the end of about 10 minutes, the total group is asked to consider the role
reversal and what implications it has for the group. By getting into the other person's
shoes and having to argue his side, it often becomes easier to understand diverse
points of view, and it may give those desiring to break the deadlock an opportunity
to do so honorably.

People usually argue from extreme positions. There is usually (except on issues of morality) a wide range of acceptable compromises. But, again, intensive debate and argument lead to a condition in which personal image more than personal belief or idea is being defended. To not lose becomes of greatest importance. By asking members to think of a solution which they might not like, but which would incorporate as much of the opposing position as they possibly could, they are forced to do something constructive rather than just argue and defend. Just getting the group to move in the direction of being constructive may induce the compromise and resolution that is needed. Once the group is willing to make a few concessions, the process becomes easier, and it is no longer a problem of saving face.

There are many ways of going about helping groups move off what appear to be irreconcilable positions. One way is to simply get them thinking about the other person's position and not just their own, or by inducing them to build a workable solution instead of just arguing intellectually. Most action programs represent compromise merely because many people must be satisfied.

14. The Ideal Program: Movement from Old to New Ideas

Objectives

To help give a group an avenue for creating new approaches to old problems
To legitimize the ideas of the creative person in a group dominated by individuals who feel threatened by any change in organizational direction

Setting

Change for its own sake is by no means good. It helps to have a purpose, to analyze present conditions, and to develop program alternatives that seem appropriate in light of changing objectives or conditions. A problem arises when institutions or groups want to maintain the status quo and are satisfied with the way things are going in spite of obvious limitations. The following exercise is aimed at facilitating new ideas, and it can be a constructive experience for most groups in need of reappraising their present conditions.

Action

Heterogeneous groups of from five to eight are established. They are given the seemingly impossible task of creating the ideal organization within which to work. In a group of teachers it would be a school; if administrators of an industrial plant, it would be the plant itself. The only ground rule is that they must not look at present conditions, but rather at conditions as they would like them to exist. It is suggested that they should not dwell on physical structures and material conditions, that it would be more helpful to look at the relationships and interpersonal factors that occur in the organization. Again, how would they like it to be? The very experience is freeing and allows people who have been restricted by their own roles or policies to begin thinking in terms of alternatives. Usually one hour is necessary since it is often 15 or 20 minutes before the initial outburst of energy produced by dreams and fantasies subsides.

At the end of an hour, the process is stopped, and the group is asked to look at their product to this point and to build a series of possible proposals that they believe may be feasible in the organization at the present moment. This should take an additional 45 minutes. The entire process is very diagnostic of the organization. The presentation of proposals should be limited to about 10 minutes, and questions allowed only for clarification.

It should be noted that such an experience can be very dangerous, and the exercise should not be used unless:

1. Those in positions of power within the group or organization are aware that the good feelings created by the exercise will soon turn to disillusionment and resistance if none of the proposals are acted upon. The exuberance generated from hope and the freeing of unspoken dreams can become a destructive force.
2. A mechanism is established after the presentation to ensure that some of the ideas are developed. This means making certain that accountability is built into the group.

Actually the exercise is a first step in helping a group look at the possibilities that exist in the "here and now" and realize that many of the ideas that are pushed aside as impossible can, in fact, be initiated given the appropriate climate. But, it is the climate that first must be changed.

15. The Open Chair: A Means of Insuring Greater Group Participation

Objective

To interject new ideas and opinions into a group meeting without losing the advantage of a small number of participants

Rationale

Quite often a large group (perhaps 10 to 25 members in this case) is faced with an issue that needs the involvement of all its members, but the facilitator is aware that an open discussion would probably only polarize positions and cloud the important aspects of the problem. Thus, while it is important for members to feel that their ideas are being represented in the discussion, they must feel some identification with and responsibility to the group as a whole. If those involved in the discussion can hold a responsibility to the group rather than the need to defend their own position, the chance for compromise and eventual consensus is greatly enhanced.

Setting

The large group selects a representative group of individuals to discuss the topic that is posing a problem. The smaller group of perhaps six or seven takes seats in a small circle and an extra chair is placed there. Those not directly involved take chairs on the outside of this inner circle.

Action

As the discussion develops, individuals on the outside of the circle may move to the empty chair. They may make an observation or express an opinion on either the issue (task level) or on how the discussion is being conducted (process level). Unless asked to remain for a few minutes by the inner group, the contributor then leaves the circle, and the chair is open to another interested person. This structure insures the outside members that their concerns are being represented and, as observers, they also have a better opportunity to note any personal factors that may be reducing the effectiveness of the group. This particular problem-solving structure assumes that the group is at a point in its development where it can delegate authority in a reasonable manner. It also assumes that participants would like those in the middle to resolve the problem being discussed. If this is not so, it is possible for disruptive persons on the outside to destroy the intent by dominating the inner group with personal biases or irrelevant points of view.

Exercises that are Helpful in Diagnosing Group Problems

The following three activities are designed to help in the diagnosis of group problems in a manner that will facilitate the working group in understanding its own work process and, to some degree, point toward logical solutions of issues that reduce the group's effectiveness.

16. The Newspaper Interview: A Means of Discovering the "Real" Issues in a New Group

It is true that what limits many working groups is their lack of tools or methods for solving problems and making decisions. However, just as often, the problems that prove most disruptive (and cause the greatest loss of time and energy) are the result of poor interpersonal relationships and the lack of any mechanisms for improving this human relations factor. Similarly, tensions resulting from innumerable sources can immobilize a group (and, yet, the destructive feelings generated find no legitimate outlet) indirectly through covert hostility and passivity. Here we are talking about the emotional or maintenance side of the ledger. Increasingly it is being recognized that if a group is not responsive to the emotional needs of its members as they work together, the task may never be completed.

Thus, it is necessary for groups that work together for any length of time to spend some of that time taking care of the problems that are bound to arise because of their own insensitivity to each other or simply because of their own lack of interpersonal skills. The problem is that people may willingly talk for hours about problems involving technical, task-related skills, but will avoid, even for a few minutes, looking at how the group operated on the human level. Were individuals in the group shut out of participation, did certain individuals dominate, was hostility suppressed, was problem solving shared, were the real issues raised? These and many other questions reveal how closely personal feelings are related to overall objectives. The aim is not to have the group solve all the personal problems of its members. Rather, it is to come to grips with procedures, fears, or behaviors that reduce the effectiveness of that group. In looking carefully at their own work process it is quite possible that individuals will grow personally and become more effective as members. Even more important, the group will develop a climate built on a base of honest communication, shared leadership, and a concern for its members. But, again, this deserves and requires time, effort, and a certain amount of risk. Following are a few exercises that can help a group begin to work with process skills at both a personal and a group level.

Objectives

To bring into the open issues that may influence how a group operates from the beginning
To establish an immediate climate of honesty and "leveling" among the participants

Setting

Very often when a group of people come together for the first time they bring with them an assortment of feelings, concerns, and expectations that may influence their participation for some time. It is very important to help clear the air from the beginning, to find out where the group is, and to give people an opportunity to express themselves. This particular exercise is more effective with a group of over 10 (ideally 20 or more) and as many as 100. From the large group, the facilitator selects a random group of "reporters"—enough for one reporter in every group of seven or eight. These individuals should be brought together while the larger group is still milling around waiting for the beginning of the program (allow 10 minutes). The facilitator gives the following directions to reporters:

You each represent a different newspaper.

It is your task to interview a group of about seven or eight of these people and find out as much as you can about them- as a group and as individuals. Names are not important, but you may wish to find out:
Why are they here? What do they expect to get out of the meetings?
Do they have any reservations about coming?
Outside of the stated reasons for the group being together are there any particular hidden goals different members have that they would like to share?
Do they have any doubts, suspicions, or special concerns about the meetings, and how they are going to be conducted?
If they could wish for one thing during this period of time together what would it be?
You should feel free to pursue any line of questioning you like and to use these questions as guidelines. After about twenty minutes of interviewing, you will be asked to synthesize your findings and report to the larger group. It is doubtful that there will be time to hear a full report, so please give only that information not presented by other reporters or that which is particularly important for your group.

Action

After a general introduction, the facilitator suggests that one way the members can become acquainted rapidly is by taking part in a brief exercise that will clarify the purposes and focus on the expectations of the group. He then quickly organizes the group into sets of about seven or eight (so as to break up any cliques). Once in groups, the participants are told that they are to be interviewed by the local press and that it will be important for them to give the press the cooperation they need. They will not be quoted by name so they should be free to express any of their concerns or feelings about this meeting. The interview will last about 20 minutes, and then each reporter will share his findings with the large group.

During the reporting session it is important that the facilitator does not allow one or two reporters to dominate the session. A reporter gives a piece of information on a point, then the next reporter speaks on that point. It is helpful to have the points being made recorded on newsprint so that they afford immediate visibility for the group. Most of the information will be obtained in about 15 or 20 minutes. It is at this point that a general overview of the program should be developed by those in charge. Considerable effort should be made to link this presentation to the expressed concerns of the group. It is possible that a brief discussion about an issue or two may prove necessary. Thus, the major reason for this activity is to help express a norm of openness and allow the participants to express their feelings and expectations. Once expressed, they can be related to the actual plans and may be used by the organizers to alter some of them.

17. The Process Diagnosis: A Means of Altering Group Behavioral Patterns

Rationale

Most groups are suspicious about being observed or looking at their own patterns of operation. People fear "getting it in the neck" and seldom have really experienced constructive criticism that does not degenerate into personally evaluative comments. Part of the problem, of course, is that most participants simply do not know the many possible ways a group can look constructively at its own work process and not feel personally threatened. It is only after a while that most groups begin to feel better about the notion of process and begin to welcome it as an integral part of any meeting. This exercise will assist a group to diagnose the factors that are both facilitating and inhibiting members in their efforts at problem solving.

Objectives

To help establish a desire in the group to process its own behaviors and procedures, to look at what happened, how people felt, what helped or hindered movement on goals
To present explicit information about how the group is operating without becoming personal and focusing on any single individual
To help the group look at alternative operating procedures, thus introducing a degree of organizational flexibility that might not have been present

Setting

This exercise is directed primarily at relatively small (5 to 18) working groups who need and desire to maximize the use of time and available resource personnel. This type of experience should not be imposed on a group by the well-intentioned facilitator. The diagnosis format and reviewing of data should be explained in detail before it is attempted. Usually if the group is concerned about maximizing its working efficiency and if there is the assurance that the diagnosis looks at group behavior rather than individual behavior, there will be a curiosity to proceed. Although most people fear looking at their own or group behavior, it also has a fascination for them, and they will be willing to experiment if the risks are not too high. If possible, this exercise should be conducted after a period of work. The collection and analysis of the data along with the report back to the group takes between 45 minutes and one hour. Time must also be left for discussion. In all, the facilitator should figure on 1½ hours (in this example six questions are used, but three might be enough). The key to success in this exercise appears to be:

1. Making certain that the questions are not too threatening.

2.   Presenting the data in an objective fashion and letting the group sort out the implications.
3.   Leaving the group with the feeling that an expert is not necessary to carry out this type of process analysis.

Action

Having agreed that they would like to participate in the diagnosis, members are (*a*) given a brief questionnaire or (*b*) asked the questions directly from newsprint charts on the board. The latter approach seems to promote a feeling of less secrecy and allows data to be transferred directly to the board. However, if trust is a real problem in the group, the questionnaire tends to give a greater feeling of security and confidentiality (the facilitator should state as casually as possible that the responses will be completely anonymous). The diagnosis is aimed at painting a more descriptive picture of the group, which is not often available in a discussion. It usually takes about 15 minutes to answer the questions. Then, while the data are being tabulated and posted for presentation and discussion, a number of options are open to the facilitator. He may suggest that the group break into trios and discuss a particular question on how the group operates and what implications there may be in the various responses. Or he could have the members (again in subgroups) discuss the kinds of behaviors in this group and others they have noticed that reduce participation and increase defensiveness on their part and in others. The posting takes about 20 minutes, and the task during that period should be process-oriented and directed in a manner that will lead to more rather than less openness in the subsequent discussion. Following are six questions that exemplify a wide range of possible questions that could develop important data. All of the data from them can be easily tabulated and visually presented to the members for their own interpretation.

Question 1

Indicate which of the diagrams best represents the relations that exist among the members of this group. Place the letter A beside the figure that *you* feel most represents the group. Place the letter B beside the figure you believe most group members will choose.

Rationale for Question 1

Most people have a definite feeling about their group and how its members relate to one another and to the group as a whole. It is also true that in many groups members feel that others see the group differently than they do. If, as it is assumed, the group wishes to maximize its working relationships and it is discovered that most of the members respond to the number that refers to subgrouping, then the group

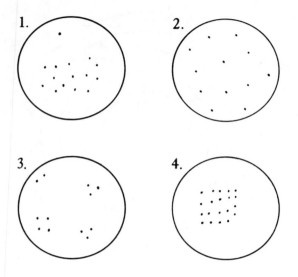

must face the implications of this in its decision-making efforts. If some members of the group see it as a group of individuals (diagram 3), it is likely that there is considerable blocking and that active or passive hostility is being generated as members attempt to win "points" for themselves, while failing to work for the benefit of the group. Further, a group that sees itself dominated by a single personality may well wish to explore means of reducing such dependency-building relationships (1). Finally, a discrepancy between what individual members think and what they feel others think about the existing pattern of relationships can provide an important reality test for a group.

Question 2

In this group a person who feels that he has the greatest possible influence and respect in the decision-making process would place himself at 1 in the circle. A person who feels he has no influence at all in this group would place himself at 7 in the circle. Place an A at the point in the circle where you feel that you belong. Place a B where you believe the group will tend to respond to the question.

Rationale for Question 2

People need to have influence; to feel impotent and remain in the group is seldom tenable. Thus, individuals often rank themselves higher in this particular question

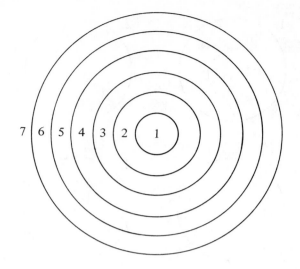

than they see others. It is an important discrepancy, for example, if all 12 members of a group see themselves in the first four circles, while 6 of the members saw the group tending to have very little influence (points 5, 6, 7). Also, the second question supplements the first question. For example, in the first question, if members see the group dominated by a single person, or if they see a sharply divided series of subgroups, they would have to explain the discrepancy if most of the group felt influential. Also, if four or five members of the group feel they have considerable influence and another four or five (or even one or two) feel they have virtually none, then there is almost inevitably going to be tension and nonproductive behavior (withdrawal, defensiveness, dispute) as those being controlled try to cope with their own feelings of impotency. Again, it is for the group to interpret the data and for the facilitator to make them aware of the evidence so that they can raise the most helpful questions.

Question 3

In a perfect group a person is able to say almost anything he thinks or feels as long as it is not totally irrelevant or destructive. Mark an A on the diagram at a point that represents how free you feel in communicating with the group. Place a B at the point you feel most members of the group will respond to the question.

1	2	3	4	5	6	7	8	9	10

No openness   Some openness,   Completely
(group closed;   moderate freedom   open and free
no freedom to speak)   to speak   to speak

Rationale for Question 3

When the data are presented in graphic form, it is difficult to avoid certain implications. For example, a wide difference in the perception of the openness that exists immediately suggests that certain members are more open than others which, in turn, implies an issue of control and raises some of the questions suggested previously. As in the other questions, it is important to explore the difference between how individuals perceive themselves in the group and how they perceive the group responding to the question. It is possible to compare individual and group averages in this and the previous question and, if desired, deviations from the mean. However, most of the implications will be quite visible when charted.

Question 4

Suggest two reasons that keep this group from being as productive as it might be when working together.

Rationale for Question 4

All groups have problems working together, and those unable to recognize some rather specific conditions that need to be improved probably are not very involved (a problem in itself) or are not being quite honest. Human relations problems are part of the game and to be expected. The only real problem occurs when the group does not face them and try to remedy them. This question is strictly designed to get some of the issues out on the table so that the group can begin to deal openly with them. Resolution will probably not come in this session, although the mere mention of some problems will go a long way toward solving those problems. The responses to this question should be integrated to some degree so that members can see which areas seem to be of most concern. Thus, instead of recording all 24 responses of a group of 12, there may be 6 or 8 that can be identified in terms of importance (i.e., the number of members who mentioned it) and noted next to the statement. Of course, a point mentioned only once may represent an important issue others were afraid to mention and therefore should be given equal time for exploration.
Note: If the participants have numbered their questionnaires or responses, there can be some interesting comparisons between responses made to the first three questions and those on this question. However, one must also be careful not to overwhelm the group with data. There is just so much that can be digested at one time.

Question 5

What are two of the best qualities of this group?

Rationale for Question 5

A person or a group grows not only by strengthening its limitations but also by maximizing its good qualities. Seldom do we take time to focus on these character- istics. The simple expression of these strengths can give a group the lift needed to deal effectively with its limitations. It may also be a first step in legitimizing praise, which is crucial in any effort to describe clearly the nature of the working group.

Question 6

What behaviors do you feel occur in groups with which you work (not necessarily this one) that you personally find annoying and disturbing to the progress of the group?

Rationale for Question 6

It is quite possible that group members are not able to face some of the issues hindering progress. By focusing upon other groups, members may indirectly raise problems that may have direct implications and that may be used as a source for diagnostic questions at a later time. Most important, the group may wish to build some preventative measures into its own operations to make certain that some of these problems do not occur.

Conclusions

The questions are diagnostic in nature, and, although some of the statements imply solutions, the data should basically be used to establish a desire to look toward solutions. If steps are not taken to resolve some of the problems raised, if the new awareness and facing up by the group is not matched by an effort to develop more effective problem-solving and communication patterns, the exercise may introduce a period of disenchantment and increased tension. Thus, again, the group and those in a position of influence must desire not only to *look* but also to *do*. As in any problem-solving situation, this will take time and energy away from other issues. However, in the long run, the time should prove beneficial to the entire work process.

18. Maslow's[5] Hierarchy of Needs: A Means of Understanding the Problem of Creating Open Communication and Feedback within a Group

Objectives

To help a group begin to understand the kinds of restraints inhibiting individual members
To focus on the emotional aspects of group process
To provide a theoretical frame of reference for understanding the group process

Rationale

According to Maslow, individuals tend to pass through certain stages of development, and the focus of their needs tends to change. How a person acts in a variety of situations will depend partly on the demands and uniqueness of the present moment and partly on the general developmental level in which the individual is functioning. It is not that we ever are able to satisfy all of our needs; in fact, even as mature adults many are still unsatisfied. The point is that as we mature developmentally, from childhood, through adolescence, and through adulthood, the focus of our needs and our inability to see beyond them changes. Thus, the first year or so of a baby's life is dominated by physiological needs. But, even though a preoccupation with such things as food, water, and sex are brought under rational control, there are times when even the most mature individuals feel the overpowering push of some physiological need. Similarly, the growing child is often overly concerned about the safety of his environment. Whether he is safe from harm or threat can prove to be a dominant theme in his developmental system of needs. For the adult, however, familiarity and experience have provided the feeling of safety except in unusual crisis situations. Actually, it is the higher-order needs such as love and self-esteem that seem most difficult for people to handle. If these needs were met to a satisfactory degree, people would no longer have to expend a great amount of time fulfilling them at a period in their lives when they should be able to accept themselves as they are and concentrate on developing their own potentials.
On p. 126 is the well-known Maslow diagram of hierarchical needs.

Theoretically, a person moves upward with a tendency to satisfy one level of need before tackling the next. It is a rare person who feels fulfilled in the areas of love and self-esteem. How few are the people who are able to give and accept love and feel unconditionally accepted. Even fewer have resolved the needs to dominate and control, to achieve and be important.

[5]Maslow, A. H., *Motivation and Personality,* New York: Harper and Row, 1954.

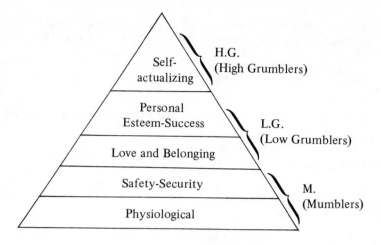

Setting

In any group there are individuals who are controlled to some degree by their own needs in one of these areas. The person who blatantly says, "Why can't we be open here and just say what we really feel?" is either completely unaware of the forces restricting an individual's ability to be open or is sending up a smoke screen to hide his own apprehensions. Personal needs act as an important inhibiting factor in the communication and development of any group. This is in itself neither good nor bad, merely an important reality. When individuals within a group push too rapidly for openness, being personal, and giving freely of feedback, it may lead to considerable pain as the group struggles to protect itself from itself. People do not wish to be rejected or to fail in a particular task. Thus, most will play it relatively safe. Sometimes it is important to help a group gain new respect for the various levels at which people operate. If such is the case, then this exercise may provide some insights. This particular activity assumes that the facilitator is in some sort of authority role and wields considerable influence. It also assumes that he is willing to be open about his own role and willing to alter his own behavior if it will benefit the functioning of the group.

Action

The group is broken into trios to discuss quite specifically the role of the facilitator, his strengths and limitations (with examples), and how he might improve his role in ways that would facilitate the working of the group. After the initial groan, an unusually loud and animated discussion usually takes place with nearly everyone participating and sharing ideas. There is no doubt that they are dissecting the facilitator, and probably enjoying it. It is essential to remind them that they need to be specific on all counts. After 10 or 15 minutes (hopefully that will be enough) the facilitator stands by the board and asks the group to list the limitations that were being discussed with such zest. It is quite possible that no one will volunteer. Those comments that are made will tend to be rather vague and indirect unless the facilitator's rapport with the group is unusually good. Even when asking for good points or ways in which his performance could meet the group's goals, the discussion will probably drag, with few individuals participating.

Discussion and Reference to Maslow's Theory

It is important to reaffirm the significance of the discussion and the data presented (hopefully the facilitator will take notes and expand on them). But, it is also clear that the discussion lacked something vital that was present during the discussions in the trios. If possible, the group should develop reasons for the obvious change in spontaneity and involvement. There are many possible reasons: fear of being evaluated by the facilitator or other members, discomfort in making direct criticism (for fear of getting it back), the leader-subordinate relationship that exists, and, perhaps, the fact that it is easier to be candid with two or three rather than the whole group.

At this point it is helpful to give a brief description of Maslow's theory of needs and how it relates to the behaviors that people are willing to exhibit. It seems to be true of most groups that when individuals do not like something about how the group is being conducted, sense becomes the better part of valor, and a disgruntled "mumble" is the most that rises to the surface. Some individuals will actually "grumble" to another person or to the group about what is happening, but it is the rare person who will take the bull by the horns and do something about the situation. This condition is particularly obvious in many classrooms where a teacher may be ineffective or not meeting the needs of the students, and yet nothing is said or done. The same is true with the boss. To say something places the person in jeopardy of losing the boss's good graces and losing his own esteem because of reaction in the job (an even lower level need). As a result, people tend to mumble (see M. on diagram) or grumble (L.G. = Low Grumble), but few are willing to pay the potential price and say it as it is (H.G. = High Grumble). High grumblers in a group are usually either those who have worked through their own needs and feel accepted and secure (self-actualizing level) or individuals who are striving for personal recognition (often need for esteem). The two types are easily recognized by the group, and although examples should not be made, it is useful to suggest that the general categorizing of needs and subsequent performance is limited. The theory does, however, raise an important question. How can a group climate be developed that minimizes the threat to personal needs and helps open up a free expression of opinions and ideas? The facilitator may wish to explore this question in a variety of possible ways, or he may choose to let the implications go for a future discussion.

7

exercises in group development: understanding characteristics of the well-functioning group

1. *Creating a Theory of Group Development from Experience*   This exercise assumes that the groups have been involved in a developmental process over an extended period of time. If such is the case, this activity will help members think conceptually about group development both in the context of their own group and in relation to other groups.

2. *Tower Building*   This exercise is a highly realistic organizational task involving participants in a process that focuses on: (*a*) the development of specific communication patterns, (*b*) the identification of various roles, (*c*) the use of decision making (on several occasions), and (*d*) membership criteria in a task-oriented group. Underlying all of this is the fact that the simulation activity enables a group to move through many of the stages of development in an intense but brief period of time.

3. *The Bag or the Box: The Stress of Ambiguity upon the Development of a New Group*   As in many of the previous exercises, the participants are placed in a situation that exaggerates the kinds of tensions and ambiguities found in any new group. How a new group copes with such tensions and ambiguities is demonstrated in a situation in which: (*a*) leadership roles are not clarified, (*b*) appropriate behaviors are not defined, and (*c*) a problem is present, but no clues as to method are provided.

4. *The Medical Emergency Task: The Use of Consensus in Decision Making*   Participants are placed in groups of six to ten members and provided with a time-pressured task in which there is a correct response (procedural rating task). For the group to have the best possible response, it is essential that members discover those in the group who actually have the most knowledge of the task. Learnings are derived from the way the group develops and what human factors deter it from doing as well as it might. A clear measure of objectivity is gained because the data are quantifiable, and one is able to determine the degree to which the group uses its resources effectively.

Almost all of the exercises outlined in this section could be used as a means to help focus on a single aspect of group activity. What is unique about the design of these activities is that they clearly draw out so many behaviors and create such varied demands. Thus, they are ideal if the facilitator wishes to explore with the group the total perspective of its development as well as the manner in which such things as norms, goals, problem solving, leadership, and membership interlock and form a single picture defining where the group is at that moment in its growth. Occasionally such designs are effective when introducing a new group to the concepts of group process and to the kinds of pressures that help determine behavior. More often, however, the learnings that can be cultivated from these experiences will be more easily grasped if the group has a previous understanding of the different components which together determine the process of a particular group.

One reason why it is difficult for a new group to grasp some of the important implications in its activities is that members simply cannot sort out the variety of experiences and behaviors that are occurring and then piece them together as part of an interacting whole. Equally important is the need for skilled observers. It is not unusual for three observers to be assigned to a group of eight or ten during one of these activities. It is most important that they have had enough experience and have developed enough skills to capture the many subtle aspects of behavior that blend together to determine the existing climate in the group and its particular stage of development. Since the observers are usually members of the larger participant group, a certain sophistication and experience in understanding group process is assumed.

1. Creating a Theory of Group Development from Experience

Objectives

To explore the developmental aspects that seem to occur in most groups
To help the participants think conceptually and to organize their learnings into a meaningful and systematic analysis of groups and their development

Setting

This activity will be explained in terms of (*a*) an ideal and (*b*) the average or common situation.

Ideal: The study of groups should ideally be done over a period of time that allows individual participants to internalize their insights from experience and practice within a developing conceptual framework. Learning about groups is often facilitated when individuals are placed with members they do not know and over a period of weeks asked to participate together in different tasks. Given time and a variety of experiences together, a certain pattern of development will begin to be evident. This will be especially true if the group is expected to work toward goals that they must decide, to make decisions in light of the decision-making procedures that they create, to generate participant roles as a result of the changing needs of the group, and to establish patterns of communication and leadership that reflect these changing needs. Such leaderless groups are able to develop important understandings about group process if a facilitator is available occasionally to help them look closely at a particular issue or concept that they might not naturally focus on without assistance. Thus, a few hours a week over a period of several months can be most helpful in developing a clear perspective of group development. This, of course, is not to say that intensive time blocks together are not also valuable, only that it is difficult to grasp the significance of all that is happening in a short time period.

Average: Most often it seems that groups do not have the time to gain a conceptual understanding of how groups operate. They are most often brought together for a short (perhaps intensive) period, and it is hoped that they "get something out of it."

This particular exercise is aimed more particularly at groups that have had the opportunity to work and learn together and those that have some understanding of what to look for in terms of the process of working groups. For the purpose of this example, it is assumed that three small groups have worked together over a period of weeks both as a single large group in some activities and as individual work groups of perhaps seven to nine members.

Step 1. Three new groups of from seven to nine participants are created. They are composed of two or three members from each of the old working groups. The facilitator gives the three groups the following task:

> As a group, look over your experiences of the past several months (weeks, days) and develop a theory of group development that may be applied to many new groups as their members work over a period of time to become effective problem solvers. Are there particular stages of development that most new groups seem to move through? Can certain behaviors be expected from the members? You will have sixty to ninety minutes to build your group development theory and present it back to the total group (all three groups in this case) in some graphic manner. For example, you may wish to present your ideas using pictures, you may wish to develop a skit, or you may design another method for transferring your ideas to the other participants.

Note: It is very important that the groups have enough time, since the tendency is that they will spend considerable time discussing what has happened to them in their own groups and little time attempting to integrate it into a theoretical framework. Thus, at the end of 45 minutes, the groups should be warned that they have only about 20 or 30 minutes to complete their task and be ready to make their presentation. This usually leads to the same kinds of problems that arise in most decision-making groups under pressure—forced decisions and reduced participation.

Step 2. At the end of the hour or hour and a half, the groups are asked to make their presentation. It is important to keep the presentations to no more than 10 minutes and preferably closer to 5. (They should be made aware of this during their planning since it pressures them to make a more precise presentation.) At the end of this time it is most helpful for the facilitator to integrate many of the ideas presented and to supplement them with theoretical concepts about development with which he is familiar and which seem appropriate to the discussion.

Step 3. The three groups that started the day and from which the three theories were generated are reconvened. They are given 30 minutes to process their own work together. The group discusses what they saw occur and how they feel about it. They also may wish to analyze what happened in terms of the theory developed from the total resources of the three groups. They are also asked to compare the new groups with the performance of their old groups.

Step 4. Briefly, the three groups are asked to share with the total groups any learnings they gained from the last discussion. The facilitator may wish to explore how many of the characteristics of long-term group development can be seen in the initial phases of a new group in a problem-solving situation.

Variation

With a group that is interested in group process but has not worked together previously, it is possible to give the same instructions suggesting that they look at groups with which they have worked in the past. It has been found that they too hold keys to useful theory, and they will also generate important data within their work group that can later be analyzed in terms of the theory that is developed.

2. Tower Building[1]

Objectives

To aid a group in focusing on the aspects of helping within the context of a particular task
To alert a group to the problems that may develop when working under severe pressures (in this case time and competition)
To deal directly with the inhibiting norms, roles, and leadership practices that can minimize the use of the group's resources

Setting

This exercise is as close to real life as one can get and still remain in the laboratory concept. It involves all the important aspects of group planning and decision making, such as the allocation of human and material resources, working agianst time deadlines, altering strategies in the face of unexpected crisis, and seeing the problems inherent in negotiations. It provides an opportunity to view the evolution of conflict and compromise as it exists in many working groups, particularly if they have not developed skills in group problem solving.

From 2½ to 3 hours should be allowed for this exercise. It can be undertaken with as few as 12 participants divided into two groups (two observers and two groups of five). However, the activity generates greater excitement and involvement among

[1] The idea for this exercise was originally developed by Clark Abt in his simulation activity, "An Education System Planning Game," originally played in 1965 at Lake Arrowhead, Calif.

the participants if there are four or six groups with from seven to nine members and an observer or two in each group. It should be noted that, given space, materials, and an effective communication system, virtually any even number of groups can participate (on one occasion the authors witnessed 20 groups with 200 students and teachers enthusiastically involved for 3½ hours). As in many of the other exercises that focus on the dimensions of group process, it may prove interesting and enjoyable for groups unsophisticated in group analysis, but many of the potential learnings will pass them by. Participants with at least an understanding of basic group concepts will take considerably more away from the exercise. The following description is based on four groups of seven members each, with an observer in each group. The room should be large enough for each group to meet with some privacy. In most cases heterogeneous groups seem to be especially effective.

Action

After the large group has been divided into four groups of equal size (some stratification may be necessary if groups are to be truly heterogeneous), the facilitator says:

> You are a group of architects [each group] who have won one of four contracts to build a tower. Although your tower will be built independently of the other three, it is to be judged in competition with the others. There is to be a planning deadline and a construction deadline. The criteria to be used in judging the four towers include height, beauty, strength, and message [symbol or motto, etc.].A prize will be distributed to each of the three best towers. Independent judges will appraise the towers, and their decisions will be final.
>
> Your groups now have thirty minutes to develop a diagrammatic plan of the tower you are going to build. You should know that you will have to plan in terms of certain materials which will be made accessible to you only during the building phase. The judges will also be asked to consider the completeness of this initial plan in their overall judging. The materials available for building will include [for each group] :
> 2 rolls of masking tape (1″ wide)
> 2 rolls of colored streamers
> 1 pair of large scissors
> 1 ruler
> 1 roll of colored toilet paper
> 150 sheets of medium newsprint (36″)
> 4 magic markers (different colors)
> 12 large sheets of construction paper (different colors)
> It may be possible to negotiate with other groups for certain additional materials. Also, other materials from the person of the participants may be used; however, no artificial bases, for example from chairs, wastebaskets, etc., may be used. The tower must stand alone on its own support- it may not be attached from the ceiling.

You may begin your planning. Since this is a competitive situation, no additional directions will be given during the planning period.

After 25 minutes of the planning period, the following announcement is made to the four groups.

We are disappointed to have to announce that because of the existing crisis in government funding, we have not been allocated all of the materials we originally anticipated. As a result, there are only enough materials available for building two towers. We are extremely sorry for this inconvenience. Rather than selecting two groups from the plans developed at this stage, we have decided to allow two groups to merge, decide on one plan, and build a tower together. Thus, there will be two towers each constructed by two teams from a plan on which they both agree. You will have an additional thirty minutes planning time to integrate your ideas or to come up with a new plan. Remember, both teams must agree on the final plan [the facilitator selects the teams that are to join forces].

After 30 minutes, the following announcement is made.

You now have thirty minutes to build your tower. It must be completed by _____ at which time the judging will take place. Remember the criteria of height, beauty, strength, and message. The judges will also circulate among the groups to make certain that all regulations are being followed. Good luck.

Observation and Data Collection

There are four major sources of information that will be discussed with the participants.
1. There is information gained by the observer during the initial planning phase. He will find it most useful to focus upon a few salient features of the groups such as: (a) communication pattern (who to whom), (b) leadership styles exhibited, (c) specific behaviors that seem to inhibit or facilitate the group during the planning.
2. The second planning session provides another distinct period of observation. One of the observers should collect the same type of data gathered during the first observation period, except now on the combined groups.
The other observer should turn his attention to the developmental aspects of the new combined group. This should be carried through the actual construction period. For example, he might ask the following questions as he observes the groups:

a. How is the potential leadership conflict either resolved or not resolved?
b. What norms are developing within this group, and are they different from those that existed in the original smaller group you observed?
c. Have individuals with certain roles in the first group taken new ones in the larger group, and, if so, what is their reaction to this state of affairs?

    d. How is the decision-making process developed in this second planning session? Is consensus actually reached, or is one plan forced on the total group? What are the responses of the group members? How is resistance exhibited (actively or passively)?

    e. Is there a real attempt to involve members from both groups through the allocation of responsibility during the building phase? How?

3. During the actual building phase, both observers should concentrate on the questions in *b* above. Special attention should be given to the quality of participation of the various group members. Is there any difference in the quality of participation among those in leadership (control) roles and those less involved in the planning? Are there signs of withdrawal and resistant behaviors by certain members? Can these behaviors be explained as a result of the historical development of the two groups, i.e., the merger?

Do the two groups tend to work together as one, or are the original relationships developed before the merger still the basis for most communication and participation during the building stage?

4. The final source of data is collected from a reaction sheet handed to all participants at the time the tower is finally completed. Information from this instrument will be used by the facilitator in a summary of the activity. This may provide a wide range of data. Below are a number of questions that might be useful for a summary discussion.

Please note the letter of the original planning group you joined. Group A B C D

My opinions were valued and solicited in the first planning group. (circle one)

1	2	3	4	5	6	7
Not at all			Some			Completely

My opinions were valued and solicited in the second planning group.

1	2	3	4	5	6	7
Not at all			Some			Completely

If there was a difference in the problem-solving climate that developed in one group, briefly explain why.

How satisfied are you with the product of your merged group?

1	2	3	4	5	6	7
at all			Somewhat			Completely

What specific behaviors hurt your group's (merged) efforts to work together and be as successful as it might have been?

What behaviors were facilitative as the two merged groups attempted to work together?

Judging and Discussion Period

Immediately after the towers have been completed, a period of about 20 minutes is taken to (*a*) have participants complete the brief reaction sheet, (*b*) have about a 10-minute break, and (*c*) have the judges (a team of three) decide on the winning tower. The winner and prize are not announced until after the discussion period.

JUDGE'S EVALUATION SHEET
On a one- (low) to-seven (high) scale, rate the towers on the following criteria.

	Height	Beauty	Strength	Message	Total
Team One (A & B)					
Team Two (C & D)					

After the break, each merged team (A & B and C & D) meet together to discuss what happened. It is assumed that during the break the two observers compared notes and have agreed upon a procedure for processing what occurred during the planning session prior to merging as well as the one after the two teams had to join forces.[2] If the group is helped with stimulating questions about what happened as the participants worked together, the discussion should require at least 45 minutes. Special attention should be given to the behaviors or situations that helped or did not help the two groups merge into a working team.

Summary

During this discussion, the facilitator should be organizing the data from the participant reaction sheets. His 10- or 15-minute presentation of these data should underline the learnings being discussed in the two groups. He should be free to draw both inter- and intragroup hypotheses from the data and then be willing to ask for con-

---

[2] If time allows, it is usually very helpful for the facilitator to spend as much as 30 minutes (prior to the exercise) with the observers, giving them the sequence of events and their role in the post-session processing. It is important that they interject their process data as a stimulus for further discussion and underline a point being made in the group. They should not just report data and await a reaction.

firmation or denial of his views. This type of presentation and discussion can help show the importance of reaction sheets and process periods after a period of problem solving and group involvement.

Conclusion

A natural end to the exercise is to report the judges' results. This can be done with humor and zest. If possible, the winning team can be given a prize that is easily divided (Cokes, etc.) while the losers receive a booby prize that can also be divided (large candy bar, etc). Occasionally, this award period offers new information for discussion.

3. The Bag or the Box: The Stress of Ambiguity upon the Development of a New Group

Objectives

To demonstrate the impact of an ambiguous and potentially threatening environment on a developing group
To observe the building of tension-reducing mechanisms within a climate of heightened anxiety

Rationale

Individuals or groups, when placed in unfamiliar surroundings and faced with unpredictable variables, will tend to become disoriented. They will then organize that environment in a manner that is safest for them at that moment. Under these conditions, leadership behavior becomes exaggerated and dependency magnified as the group struggles to bring order and predictability to their situation. It is rare in our experience that we are in a position to stand back and observe a group under such stress—usually we are too much involved to even recognize what is happening. Once having observed it in others, there is a tendency, however, to become more aware of similar conditions developing and of our responses to them.

Setting

This is one of the few exercises that requires special physical conditions. It is included because of its increasing availability and the willingness of facilitators to use it. Of first importance is to secure an observation room with a one-way viewing mirror. This room should be large enough to hold 15 or 20 people. Also, the participants' room should be large enough to allow movement. (In most cases this would rule out observation rooms used by counselors). A small circle of seven to ten chairs is placed at one end of the room. If possible, the participants should be a group of from seven to ten students (preferably boys and girls) between about nine and twelve years of age.[3] While it is not necessary that the children be unacquainted, it is best that there is some heterogeneity in the group and that relationships are, to some degree, still evolving.

Action-Directions

The group of students are met outside the observation room and told simply that they are to enter the room and work as a group for the next 30 minutes. They are requested not to leave the room.

When they enter the room, they find a variety of conditions that will tend to be disorienting. First, there will be no authority figure to give them directions or specific written directions to follow. Second, there will be the one-way mirror and the suspicion that they are being observed. Finally, there will be an object in one corner (at some distance from the circle of chairs). The object will be either a large canvas bag with a person in it (covered) or a blanket with a person under it. The person does not move or make any sound. On other occasions a large box may be used which is made to resemble a cage. In it sits a person (apparently unable to get out) who does not speak or move. A sign on the cage suggests only "Do not move."

Directions to Observers

As in many new groups or in ongoing groups faced with an anxiety-producing situation, the developmental process will be influenced and a certain amount of regression is predictable. Those observing should note the specific tension-reducing behaviors used by individuals within the group and by the group as a whole. Questions such as the following may be helpful to the group as it observes the unfolding events:

How is the potential leadership in the group identified?
How do these leaders orient themselves to: (a) the lack of structure, (b) the bag, and (c) the mirror?
How do they orient themselves to the group?
What conflicts seem to arise because of the uncertainty of the situation?
How are these conflicts resolved or at least reduced?

[3] It should be noted that children are suggested for this exercise because they are so spontaneous. with their responses. Adult participants respond similarly, but less dramatically and less overtly. The young students also provide an interesting change of pace for the usually adult-centered groups and give them a new perspective on group development.

What are the various individual and group roles that tend to develop as the participants attempt to cope with the anxiety-producing situation?
Are particular rules of behavior perceived as acceptable by the group (norms), and do these change during the 30-minute observational period?
Does the group move through definable stages as it attempts to cope with the ambiguity and make sense out of the unfamiliar environment?

Interview

Following the 30 minutes, the children should be given an opportunity to move into the observers' room and watch the observers as they move into the room with the bag. Perhaps with Cokes and in the most relaxed and informal atmosphere, groups of observers and children may discuss what happened. The participants are bound to have many feelings, and it takes skill, patience, and real interest to draw these out. Many of the questions which the observers have been asking themselves can now be broadened to include the perspective of the children. It is important to note, however, that the children may have many questions of their own and it may be helpful to give them a chance to ask them so that the process becomes one of exchanging ideas and less like the typical adult-student interrogation. The "bag" should also respond to questions from the students as a means of breaking the ice during the interview period. At some point the person should be allowed out of his bag and allowed to participate, although on several occasions, after a period of questions by the children, the authors have seen the "bag" walk out of the room.

Post-Session Analysis

Following the departure of the children, the observers should (perhaps in clusters of three or so) summarize their learnings in relation to parallel situations in other groups, particularly in terms of the process of group development. The sharing of these ideas based on concrete examples can be most stimulating.

4. The Medical Emergency Task: The Use of Consensus in Decision Making[4]

Objectives

To explore the strengths and limitations of consensus in the decision-making process
To measure the degree that resource personnel are adequately used in a particular simulation exercise

[4]This design was created by Oliver Bjorksten, M.D. and his colleagues as an alternative to Jay Hall's NASA simulation which has proven to be classic in the area of simulation designs involving the use of consensus.

To help participants use personal feedback in evaluating how effective the group has been in accomplishing the major objectives of the simulation

Background and Rationale

This type of simulation activity has provided small-group theorists interested both in research and application with a unique instrument that (*a*) allows a group to explore with some objectivity how well it uses appropriate resource people in a particular task; (*b*) provides an ideal situation for observing styles of leadership, roles, norms, and communication patterns in a relatively short period of time; and (*c*) uses data generated from the participants in a manner that is difficult to question and raises a minimum of resistance because of the nonevaluative nature of the feedback.

The game is relatively simple, but very difficult to accomplish. The idea is to provide individuals with a task that is interesting and which requires a certain expertise, but is foreign enough to most members that those participating would probably not know which individuals actually hold the most information. By using a medical emergency format, both of these conditions are met. It is left to the group to discover which individuals actually have the most expert knowledge on the subject, and then to use that knowledge in the most constructive manner. In one group, the expert turned out to be a little old lady who spent many long winter evenings exploring medical books as a means of relaxation. In another group, the expert turned out to be an eleven-year-old girl science whiz from a ghetto school who tried to sell everyone on the notion that she knew nothing. Whether a group even attempts to seek out such resource people is the first important question to be raised. More often than not there are other credentials (confidence, loudness of voice, certainty, or charisma) that become influential in solving the problem. As a result, groups seldom do as well as they might. Even the effort of the best individual in the group will not insure the best response. Thus, even though the discussion process can produce tension and arguments as the group members attempt to establish their own influence, the process itself should lead to more effective decision making.

Groups often play with the idea of consensus, but few groups have the self-discipline, patience, and interest to manage the process successfully. This exercise puts the idea of consensus to the test and reveals just what a difficult process it is.

Setting

The groups undertaking this exercise should be familiar, to some degree, with the study of small groups at work and acquainted with various group concepts. The exercise can be an interesting experience for groups at various levels, but it takes some maturity and intellectual sophistication to be able to maximize the kinds of learnings that can be drawn from this experience. Groups with from six to eight participants are ideal. If there are more than 10, it becomes difficult to provide the observation and the resulting feedback in a very efficient manner. In a group of from six to eight, withdrawal or noninvolvement cannot be blamed on size.

It is possible for one facilitator to handle as many as six groups at one session (from 2 to 3 hours). However, for every two groups there should be an individual to help with the collection and analysis of the data, and each group should have at least two observers. The exercise itself is relatively self-explanatory. The difficult part for the facilitator is organizing the enormous amount of data in a fashion that can be readily understood by the participants. Some group facilitators like to have the groups compile and analyze their own data. The authors find that such analyses tend to reduce the impact and minimize the variety of learnings that are possible. It is not that each person will remember anywhere near all of the information placed before him, but some of it will usually hit home and be absorbed.

Whenever possible, it is helpful to have at least two or three groups undertaking the task at the same time. The element of competition provides an incentive factor, and the opportunity to compare the predictably different experiences of the groups adds several dimensions to the feedback process that cannot occur when only one group is involved. However, as the following text indicates, a single group can generate enough information for a week of discussions.

Action

The participants are seated in their groups, handed the individual decision form (Form A, see page 141) and asked to read it to themselves. The facilitator may wish to read this form aloud and embellish on it in ways that might stimulate interest and motivation. The participants are then requested to complete the form by themselves and without sharing their responses with anyone else. As individuals have completed this task, one of the observers in the group asks the individual to quickly read off his responses. The observer records this information in one of the columns on the group summary sheet (see page 142) under the individual's name. This usually takes no more than 4 or 5 minutes, and the other members are asked not to talk about their ideas until all the individual responses have been recorded. At this point the groups are told that they will have 45 minutes (30 minutes is about minimal) to decide as a group the rank order of the medical process. The facilitator can establish the rules of the game by suggesting how consensus actually works. It should be noted that (1) Consensus is a participative decision-making process which depends on the acceptance by all members of an idea. All members do not have to totally agree, but it is essential that they feel committed to go along with the group on a particular idea. (2) Consensus does not use tension-reducing devices such as voting to reach hasty decisions. (3) Participants are urged to share their views fully and to stick by them. (4) Consensus is based on group acceptance, thus there should be less inclination to "prove one's point," but rather a desire to meet the needs of the group. As mentioned previously, true consensus is difficult to reach. It will be difficult in this case (and it should be stressed) since success depends on time as well as on the quality of the group's responses.

MEDICAL EMERGENCY TASK

Group _____

Name _____

You are a second-year medical student, who has had a course in emergency medicine and who is on rounds in the hospital when a nurse runs up to you and your friends and screams that a patient has stopped breathing and has no pulse. You and your friends (there are no doctors or professors with you) dash into the room of this fifty-five year-old male patient and realize that you must save this person yourselves because help is about 10 minutes away. You know all the procedures for initial care from your lectures, but you cannot remember the *order* in which to apply them. Your job now is to decide in what order to apply the following list of procedures. (Remember, speed is vital since a person cannot live very long without breathing.) Place the number 1 by the first step that should be taken, the number 2 by the second most important, and so on through the twelfth step.

		Item
6*	Place patient on a solid surface (floor, bedboard) and apply external cardiac compression at 60–80 times per minute (the heel of the hand should be placed on the lower end of the sternum just above the xiphisternum).	A
7	Observe for return of spontaneous cardiac action.	B
1	Decide whether patient is suitable for resuscitation.	C
12	Give continuous vasopressors to sustain blood pressure, if necessary.	D
2	Make the diagnosis that cardiac arrest has occurred (based on apnea, no pulse, dilated pupils, cyanosis, etc.).	E
5	Give three or four rapid mouth-to-mouth artificial respirations. Continue at 12 per minute if possible, and if help is available.	F
4	Summon help and begin resuscitation.	G
9	Alert anesthesiologists; perform tracheal intubation and institute bag breathing.	H
3	Make note of the time on your watch.	I
8	Inject Isuprel 1–2 ml. into the heart if no spontaneous activity after several minutes.	J
11	Apply external defibrillator if indicated by presence of ventricular fibrillation.	K
10	Obtain ECG to determine type of cardiac arrest (asystole or ventricular fibrillation).	L

*Correct scores.

MEDICAL EMERGENCY TASK – PROTOCOL
Group Summary Sheet
Individual Predictions

	Bob	Geo.	Dick	Al	Will	Ben	Mary	Ann	Best Poss. Score	Final Group Score	Correct Score for the Item
Item A	6_0	7_1	2_4	10_4	6_0	7_1	5_1	5_1	0	5_1	6
Item B	9_2	5_2	4_3	9_2	7_0	8_1	6_1	8_1	0	7_0	7
Item C	1_0	2_1	5_4	4_3	2_1	1_0	1_0	3_2	0	2_1	1
Item D	11_1	8_4	7_5	11_1	9_3	10_2	10_2	6_6	1	8_4	12
Item E	3_1	4_2	1_1	3_1	4_2	3_1	4_2	7_5	1	4_2	2
Item F	2_3	6_1	10_5	2_3	5_0	2_3	3_2	2_3	0	3_2	5
Item G	4_0	3_1	2_2	1_3	3_1	7_3	2_2	1_3	0	5_1	4
Item H	12_3	11_2	12_3	12_3	10_1	11_2	12_3	11_2	2	12_3	9
Item I	5_2	1_2	6_3	5_2	1_2	5_2	7_4	4_1	1	1_2	3
Item J	7_1	10_2	9_1	6_2	11_3	6_2	9_1	12_4	1	10_2	8
Item K	8_3	12_1	11_0	8_3	12_1	9_2	11_0	10_1	0	9_2	11
Item L	10_0	9_1	8_2	7_3	8_2	12_2	8_2	9_1	0	11_1	10
Sum of the discrepancies for each individual	16	20	33	30	16	21	20	30	6	21	

Group Average: $\dfrac{\text{Total discrepancy scores of all of the participants}}{\text{Divided by the total number of participants}} = \dfrac{186}{8} = 23$

Group Observers

One of the two observers should undertake a who-to-whom observation chart (see the Appendix in the textbook). Beyond this, what is observed depends on the stage of the group's development. With a group that often works together, it is probable that the observers will record data that are different from might be recorded for a group that had never been together. Basically, their job is to develop behavioral data to supplement the information gained by means of the objective measures. This may be nothing more than noting behaviors that inhibit open communication or cause individuals to withdraw from active participation. In one group, leadership may be the most relevant area around which to develop observations, while in another it may be membership. The exercise is adaptable to a wide range of training needs.

Immediately after a group has successfully completed the assigned task, each member is given a copy of the Participant Questionnaire (see page 144) which he is to complete and return to the facilitator or one of the observers. It is important at this time not to let the group break away from the work situation. After an hour of intensive work together, it is easy to develop a lively discussion. This can be done by merely having individual members share some of their responses to the questionnaire, or by having the observers share some of their data. The latter approach is less constructive since there is a tendency for observers to take over and even overwhelm the members with their data. The main point here is that the groups are brimming with feelings and concerns, many of which would be lost if the natural inclination for a break were followed. This discussion can easily last 30 minutes or more. At some natural stopping point, a 10- or 15-minute break should be called before the objective data are shared to all the groups in a general session.

Gathering and Analyzing the Data

The key to the entire exercise is the tabulation, integration, and presentation of the data taken from the groups. There are several phases to this process.

Phase 1.   The facilitator and, if necessary, a helper or two gather the Group Summary Sheets which record the individual response of each participant in each group (the participants are allowed to keep Form A). While the groups are discussing the problem and trying to reach a consensus, the facilitator arrives at a deviation score for each participant. This merely means matching the response of an individual to an item. For example, an individual may rank item C as 5 when the correct score as judged by medical experts is a ranking of 1. Or an individual may rank item D as 6 while the experts believe it should be ranked 10. Thus, it is possible to determine for each item and for each individual the deviation between the participant's score and the score the medical experts believe is correct. Obviously, if the participant and the experts have the same ranking, then there would be no deviation for that item. By adding the total number of deviation points a participant has for all 12 items it is possible to determine not only how much each individual knew about the task when compared to the medical experts, but it is also

MEDICAL EMERGENCY TASK- PARTICIPANT QUESTIONNAIRE

Group _____

Name _____

Please answer the following questions as they relate to the activity in which you have just participated.

1. To what extent were your opinions and thoughts solicited and valued by the group?

   9 Completely
   8 Quite a lot
   7 A little more than moderately
   6 Moderately
   5 Neither very much nor very little
   4 Less than moderately
   3 Only a little
   2 Very little
   1 Not at all

2. Having worked with this group for an hour, suggest three words that best describe your feelings about the group (or its members) at this point.

3. How committed do you feel toward the final product developed by your group?

   9 Completely committed
   8 Quite committed
   7 Moderately committed
   6 A little more committed than not
   5 Neither very committed or not
   4 A little more uncommitted
   3 Moderately uncommitted
   2 Quite uncommitted
   1 Not at all committed

4. How much frustration or tension did you feel as a result of other people's behaviors during the work on the decision?

   9 Completely lacking in tension
   8 Approving, not bothered
   7 Only slightly bothered by tension
   6 Aware of tension but not hindered
   5 Neither tense nor not tense
   4 A little more tense than not
   3 Moderately tense and frustrated
   2 Quite frustrated
   1 Completely tense and frustrated

5. How good was the eventual decision of the group?

   9 The best possible
   8 Quite good
   7 Moderately good
   6 A little more good than bad
   5 Neither good nor bad
   4 A little more bad than good
   3 Moderately bad
   2 Quite bad
   1 The worst possible

6. Indicate the two most influential members in the group's decision-making process during this particular task.

7. Indicate the two most knowledgeable members of your group on this particular task.

possible to discover where the individual ranks among the other members of the group. It will be noted that in the protocol presented here Bob had a deviation score of 16 points while Dick had a score nearly twice as high (or 33 points from the perfect score of 0).

By adding the total deviation scores of all eight participants (as done in the protocol) and dividing by the number of participants, one arrives at a Group Average Deviation. In the protocol that score was 23. This suggests that had the group not bothered to spend all the time in discussion and had merely taken an average of their scores (roughly similar to a simple voting procedure), then that average would have been the group response. Even at this early point in the discussion, it is evident that 40 minutes of trying to reach consensus netted the group a score of 21 (see Final Group Score on the protocol) or only two points better than had they taken a quick vote and presented an average score. This suggests that the group, for some reason(s), was not able to pool its potential resources to the best advantage. It is, of course, the purpose of the simulation to help the various groups explore some of the reasons why such things occur and why some groups tend to operate most successfully while others fail rather miserably.

Phase 2. It is also possible to determine the best possible score that the group could have had on any one item—if the members had used the best resource in their group. That is, in looking at the protocol we see that Will had the correct response for item F. He ranked the item the same as the medical experts and thus had a deviation score of 0. Theoretically, if the group had explored the question thoroughly, they had present a resource person(s) who knew what was necessary. Thus, it was possible for the group to have responded correctly to that item had they used the best resource. In this particular instance, after discussing the item, the group agreed on the ranking of 3 which was 2 points from the ideal score of the experts. By adding all of the group's best possible responses for each item, it would theoretically be impossible for the group to have scored a group score of less than 6 points since they apparently did not have the resources necessary to do a perfect job in ranking the items. Had the group used all its resources, however, it would have scored considerably better than the final score of 21 deviation points. What are the reasons why people apparently were not heard and the group was not more efficient in solving its problem?

Phase 3. From the Participant Questionnaires (provided immediately after the simulation), a number of important pieces of information can be used for presentation to the entire group. For example, in the sheet reporting data relating to group 1, it is noted that information (items 6 and 7) from the who-to-whom data is presented. This information gained from observers, as well as data from the questionnaire, is gathered for each group and presented (usually on large newsprint) to the entire group. The terrible temptation is for the facilitator to overwhelm the group with too much information. Actually, his job is to help the participants absorb only the most important information.

Some of this information should have already been presented to the individual groups by their observers, whose function is to help the participants focus on the many factors that facilitated or hindered the group in its efforts to solve the problem at hand. Emphasis on both the task and maintenance levels of group operation is essential. While it is not necessary to personalize the kinds of data generated, groups usually find the activity so stimulating that they do not mind personalizing their own experiences and feelings. While the simulation may be used to develop a rather intense session of personal feedback, most groups use the experience as a means of helping them see the group as a group and the factors that influence the decision-making process.

Analysis of the Data for the Group

After the simulation itself (about 45 minutes) and the following discussion (about 30 minutes, although it could go on for much longer), the participants are usually in need of a 10- or 15-minute break. It is during this time that the final data from the post-simulation questionnaire are tabulated and included with the other information now available to all the groups. Once the groups reassemble in the large group, it is helpful to discuss the actual correct responses and the reasons for them. While this can be done with good humor, the correct answers should not be defended by the facilitator. If the participants are not satisfied, the facilitator suggests that they (1) see their local doctor, (2) the AMA, or (3) a text on cardiac arrest. It is important to take as much time as necessary to explain the method of scoring. Without understanding the nature of the deviation scores the group data will mean nothing and the value of the entire experience will be dramatically reduced.

The Protocol and Related Data

It is not the facilitator's role to play magician and make brilliant interpretations from the data. The key is to have the data placed before the participants in such a manner that it is self-explanatory. Following is the kind of information that can be shared before the entire group. With the presentation of each set of information, more relationships may be drawn between the various groups as certain patterns tend to emerge.

Data from Group 1

1. As noted previously, the group was able to improve its final score by only two points over what it might have scored taking a superficial vote among its members. It is also noted that fully half of the people in the group scored individually better than the group scored as a whole. Theoretically, by combining the insights of eight people, the group should score better than any one of its members (except in exceptional circumstances). It is, of course, essential to discover who the individuals with the most information actually are.

2. It is important to note that of the three people who talked the most only one

(George) scored among the better half in the group. In fact, two of the individuals with the lowest scores (these low scores do not have to be reported to the group— the absence of the talkers among the good scores is enough to make the point) dominated the talk time. Similarly, for some reason, Mary, Bob and Will, who had the best scores, talked very little and were virtually not talked to at all. As might be expected, those who talked the most tend to be talked *to* the most. This was not the case with Dick who might have been providing an important maintenance role which did not require being talked back to. It may well be, however, that Dick simply spoke a great deal and had little influence with the group. One person, Ben, was talked to considerably more than he talked, and it may be that he was recognized as a special resource, but, for some reason, he failed to provide the group with the kind of information it was seeking.

Often groups place blame on those individuals who tend to dominate and, as later discovered, fail to have the information or background to warrant their amount of participation. It is equally important for the group to begin taking more responsibility for its own destiny and insuring that other members have the opportunity to invest their ideas into the discussion. Some of the blame in this situation must be placed in the hands of the quieter members who fail to share information that could be beneficial or fail to see themselves as important resources. For whatever reasons, it is essential to break a pattern of limited participation if a group is to be successful in using consensus as a tool for decision making.

3.   It is clear that the group did discover an important resource person in George, but the attention given to Ann and Dick very likely reduced the group's productivity. Both Dick and Ann were seen as having considerably more knowledge (item 8) than half of the group, and each was perceived as highly influential.

4.   A pattern emerges in which it appears that a few vociferous individuals dominated the group while others stood back and observed. This is particularly evident in the types of words used to describe the group or the experience (item 14). Half of the group (the talkers and those actively involved) used generally positive words while many of the others reflected the attitudes of most people who do not feel well regarded or potent. This is further reflected in the responses to other questions. For example, three or four members of the group felt their opinions were solicited and valued in the final decision; thus they felt little frustration in the task, while three or four others definitely felt at the opposite end of the continuum.

5.   Finally, it may be said with some certainty that although the group did not do badly in its actual level of performance, the potential for solving problems in the future would not be high. There were many unresolved conflicts beginning to emerge, a disconcerting pattern of nonlistening, and signs of competition among the more active members. In a one-hour task many of these issues can easily be shoved under the rug. In real life the issues that began to surface in the simulation all too often result in destructive behaviors among the participants as they continue to meet together and as they have no legitimate means of viewing their process with an aim at improvement.

Again, it cannot be stressed too much that as much as possible the various groups should be encouraged to draw their own implications from the data and to generalize them to other groups. It is this process that makes the simulation important in the eyes of the participants.

DATA REPORTED BACK DURING THEORY SESSION WITH ALL GROUPS

The following data gathered on group 1 will be systematically reported back. Much of the learning will depend on the skill of the reporter in making the various groups understand their own data as well as the possible variables that influenced differences among the various groups.

1. Group Score (after 40 minutes of discussion)   21
2. Group Average (average deviation score of all the participants in group 1)   23
3. Best possible score of group 1   6
4. High score (worst) = 33   Low score (best) = 16
5. The four individuals with the best scores:

> Bob = 16   George = 20
> Will = 16   Mary = 20

6. The three individuals who talked the most (taken from who-to-whom data of observer)   Dick / Ann / George
7. The three individuals who were talked to the most (also who-to-whom data)   George / Ann / Ben
8. Those in the group perceived as knowing the most (taken from questionnaire)   Ben / George / Dick / Ann
9. Those in the group perceived as having the most influence   George / Ann / Dick
10. Extent to which members felt opinions were solicited and valued (Questionnaire item 1); average score = 4.5 (three people scored 3 or below)
11. Extent to which members felt committed to final decision; average score = 5.2 (2 people scored 1 and another 2)
12. The degree of frustration felt in group; average score = 4.5 (It is interesting to note that the group split between the two extremes.)
13. How good the group decision was; average score 6.5 (all scored over 5)
14. Words used to describe the group or feelings:

> cut off   involved
> put down   participating
> not listened to   sharing
> withdrawn   open
> uninvolved   fun
> frustrated   learning
> angry   thinking

Other words used which did not tend to fall at the extremes included:
worked, time, pressure, unusual, debate, consensus.